Also by Virginia E. Pomeranz, M.D., and Dodi Schultz:
THE MOTHERS' MEDICAL ENCYCLOPEDIA

THE FIRST FIVE YEARS

A Relaxed Approach to Child Care

by Virginia E. Pomeranz, M.D.
with Dodi Schultz

Doubleday & Company, Inc.
Garden City, New York
1973

For the parents who sing to their children

ISBN: 0-385-02015-5
Library of Congress Catalog Card Number 72–96254
Copyright © 1973 by Virginia E. Pomeranz and Dodi Schultz
All Rights Reserved
Printed in the United States of America
First Edition

Contents

Introduction

(Or, Who Says It Has to Be Ironed?)

If you are a young parent—and I assume, if you are reading this book, that you are, or are about to be, one—you are doubtless aware that your local bookshop's offerings on the subject of child care are exceeded in number only by volumes bearing the title *The (fill in kind of food, time of day, or any ethnic adjective) Cookbook*. Why, then, yet another romp through the rigors of rearing preschoolers?

Mainly, because I find that, despite the proliferation of printed advice, parents are still at best confused, at worst trembling with self-doubt. And no wonder.

If a mother is nursing or planning to nurse her baby, she finds that—according to Dr. X—"the nursing mother's diet should include six servings of fruits and vegetables a day." If she is not, warns Dr. Y, "Every mother must learn to be scrupulously careful in the technique of sterilizing all feeding utensils." Either way, declares a third authority, "All babies—breast or bottle—must be burped during and after feedings."

Once she has finished stuffing herself with fruits and vegetables and begun stuffing them into the baby, Dr. Y assures her that smooth sailing is inevitably in store, at least in the feeding department: "All feeding difficulties pass by the time the child gets on to solid foods." In fact, predicts Dr. X, "by the time your baby is six months old, he will probably be eating cereal, egg yolk, and a variety of fruits, vegetables, and meats."

Of course some alarming behavior problems may arise, and when you have left off brooding about Junior's soma, you had better begin probing his psyche. "There is lots of evidence," Dr. X whispers, "that all children feel guilty about masturbation." And a distinctly antisocial life style may be asserting itself in the stamping of that tiny foot, for "temper tantrums," proclaims Dr. Z, "are the ultimate in negativism." (Which, the dictionary reveals, is not mere obstinacy but "an attitude of mind marked by skepticism about nearly everything affirmed by others.")

But Dr. Z does not want you to spend much time thinking about that prospect either; there are more important tasks, and new roles for you to play. "Begin teaching your child to print when he is around three and a half years old," for one (said child is already, presumably, familiar with the rudiments of reading). Nor should other intellectual pursuits await formal training: "Mathematics is a vital area in which your child needs stimulation in his preschool years." The ideal age for *that* to start, the good doctor adds, is three.

Is four-year-old Michael retarded because he can't count? Perhaps it's because you let him masturbate. At six months he was eating fruits and vegetables but not cereal, egg yolk, or meats; maybe that was the first clue. Very likely it all stems from an early nutritional deficiency; you distinctly remember eating only four fruits and vegetables a day while you were nursing.

All those quotations are accurate. The trouble is, the advice is not. (It is not the number of fruits and vegetables on her menu but the quantity of calcium in her diet that is important for a nursing mother. Sterilizing of feeding utensils is rarely, if ever, necessary. Some babies don't burp. Solid foods may bring new feeding problems. A six-month-old may or may not be taking one solid food, let alone five different kinds. Masturbation is perfectly normal, and only those children whose parents have been panicked by Dr. X are made to feel guilty about it. Temper tantrums are common, and not forerunners of deep-seated psychic troubles. And of course no three-year-old will suffer if he or she cannot read, write, and count; Albert Einstein didn't even talk until he was three.) It is just such well-intentioned but very misleading—and often intimidating—advice that prompts a good deal of the needless anxiety on the part of today's young parents. That that anxiety *is* unnecessary is the premise of this book.

The advice in this book is based on neither abstract theories nor intensive research, but on twenty years of dealing with parents and children. It is a distillation of what I have told, and learned from, thousands of parents—to whom I am deeply indebted for asking their questions, for reporting frankly on the practicality of my answers, and not least for their own original solutions to many common problems. From those two decades of experience has evolved what I find to be an easy, relaxed approach to the exciting challenge of shepherding your newborn infant through his metamorphosis into a delightful young person—delightful, that is, to you his parents, though not necessarily to the world at large.

Which brings me to the first of four points I think are basic.

There is no one right way to raise a child. Just as each adult is unique, so is each baby; and so is every parents-and-baby combination. You must arrive at the ways and means of coping that fit *you*—whether or not anyone else would find them suitable or reject them as ridiculous.

Having a baby, or appearing in public with an infant or small child, is tantamount to declaring open season for dispensers of advice and criticism, most of it reflecting upon the child's inheritance, your capabilities, or both. You will be told that your baby is too large or too small for his age, that he is too lightly/warmly dressed for such cold/hot weather, that he should/should not be out of/still in diapers, that he is disturbingly placid or dangerously hyperactive. (Your spouse and/or your pediatrician may, and it is devoutly to be hoped that they will, assure you that you are not a failure. Do not expect complimentary comment from anyone else.) Do not despair; do ask yourself three questions:

Am I happy?

Is my husband—or wife—happy?

Is the baby happy?

If you come up with three affirmative answers, then whatever you are doing or not doing, and whatever your child is doing or not doing, is right—no matter how naïve, stupid, uninformed, eccentric, or even bizarre it may seem to someone else.

I often think, in this regard, of a young actor I know. It is his habit to return home from the theater at 11:30 P.M., greet his wife, have a late supper, and then go into the nursery and awaken the couple's nine-month-old son. The baby wakes cheerfully, plays happily with his parents for thirty to forty-five minutes, and then goes contentedly back to sleep until eleven o'clock the next morning. All the relatives and neighbors are appalled at this unheard-of behavior. But the father loves and looks forward to this uninterrupted time with the baby, the mother is tickled that her husband enjoys the infant so much, the baby basks in his parents' love and has suffered no ill effects, and the entire family sleeps well, to an hour that fits their life style. Such a schedule might not work for everyone—but it works for them. Remember those three key questions and hark back to them when some prying acquaintance tries to set you straight.

You might also—if the advice giver is a stranger (or if you don't mind estranging a friend)—put a quick end to the torture with a deliberately curt and disconcerting rejoinder. I can assure you that if someone accosts you with, "I see he's still in diapers. He's a big boy, isn't he? How old *is* he?" and you answer, "He's eight, but he's a midget," your inquisitor will not pursue the matter further. Remarks such as, "I wouldn't put my hand in the carriage if I were you; painted fingernails seem to drive him crazy, and he bites," will also discourage advances.

A corollary to the there's-no-one-right-way tenet is that it is best to *trust your own instincts.* A good many children have reached maturity without the benefit of baby books; in other parts of the world, where the literacy rate is lower than it is in our country, a good many children still do. (Some of them grow up to become doctors, lawyers, leaders of coups d'état, and other outstanding and prestigious things.) If you react naturally in dealing with your child, you will at least be consistent. Should you make any mistakes, they will tend to be the same ones time after time; thus, the child will not be confused by wide discrepancies in your reactions to him. If you follow your own feelings one day, Dr. X's conflicting advice the next, and your mother-in-law's still different prescription the third day, your child will not know what to expect, and disorientation is likely to set in rapidly.

In short, never accept advice from anyone—including me— if it goes against your grain. No matter how sterling the theory, it will be bad advice for you, and it won't work. Neither "M.D." following a name nor an appearance on a television panel makes a dispenser of advice infallible. This doesn't mean, of course, that you need proceed entirely on instinct; I certainly hope you'll find this book helpful. But unless a piece of advice really seems reasonable to you, and you're in tune with it and feel comfortable with it—forget it.

Second basic: *always tell your child the truth*. By this I do not necessarily mean that every question must be fully answered, as if you had taken an oath on a witness stand. When your preschooler demands to know your family income, it is perfectly honest to tell him it is not his business. When a two-year-old asks whence came a new brother or sister, it is unnecessary to describe the complete human reproductive system.

But what you do say should be truthful. If he is going to get an injection, and it will hurt briefly as injections are wont to do, tell him just that; don't tell him he won't be getting it, or that it will be painless. If you make a promise, keep it—and if you make a threat, carry it out. If your child learns from infancy that you never lie, he will learn honesty by your example; he will also continue to trust you when he reaches the difficult teen years, which will be very gratifying.

That honesty should extend to expression of your feelings. No one is emotionless, and you will be giving the child a rather weird picture of the world if *you* pretend to be. He will learn—and in fact must learn—that people feel happy at times and sad at other times; that anger, gaiety, confusion, amusement, laughter, and tears are all part of the human experience. Nor should you fear admitting an error: if, for instance, you've dealt with a youngster unfairly—punishing him, say, for something of which you later learn he was innocent—you should be as quick to own up and apologize as you would expect him to be. You will find that children are remarkably forgiving; and it helps them to cope with their own feelings if they know that even their parents are fallible.

The third thing it is well to bear in mind is that *children are people—but they are not just short adults*.

People have feelings and should receive a certain amount of respect by virtue of the mere fact that they are human beings. Your three-year-old terrier will not object to being discussed in the third person while he is present; in fact, if he is like most terriers I have known, he will be positively ecstatic at hearing his name mentioned. That does not apply, however, to your three-year-old son or daughter. An adult who understands English generally does not care to be discussed as if he or she were not present; the same is true of a child who has reached the verbal level.

Similarly, I feel strongly that you should not permit a child, at this age and stage, to be so used by others. If a child is old enough to tell you how he feels, for example, he is old enough to tell someone else. When four-year-old Michael is brought to my office for a follow-up check on his tonsillitis, I do not think it appropriate to ask his mother, "How is he feeling?" I turn to Michael and ask, "How does your throat feel?" I also get more accurate information this way.

Or let's say you and little Susie are in a department store, and you are accosted by a lady who explains that she is shopping for her granddaughter, who is "just your little girl's size." The clincher is, of course, "Would you mind very much if I just tried this coat on your daughter?" Probably you wouldn't, but that isn't the question. The question is: would Susie mind? I think Susie ought to be asked, if not by the stranger, then by you—and if Susie says yes, she would mind, that ought to be that. It would be gracious of Susie to cooperate, but if there's a conflict and someone's feelings are going to be hurt—who's more important to you, a stranger or Susie?

On the other hand, remember, when you become impatient with your baby and later with your crawler and toddler, that children are *not* adults. While they may have similar feelings, their knowledge is quite *dis*similar. Upon arrival it is, in fact, nonexistent. Imagine finding yourself in a strange country, populated by persons five times your height and twenty times your weight; the houses, vegetation, furniture, in fact everything you can see, are of strange and unfamiliar contour and design; you can neither speak, read, nor understand the language; you have no sense of time. You are very hungry. And you cannot walk. If you can imagine that, you have some idea of the situation in which a newborn baby finds himself. It's not quite as terrifying as the dramatic dilemma I've described, since there are no prior memories to which to compare the present condition. And, as we know, things will improve: he will gradually learn to move about, communicate, recognize objects, and even grow to the size of the natives. In the meantime, he must do what he can to make his feelings and needs known—chiefly, at first, by crying. And he must learn all those elementary facts and concepts that are by now second nature to you. Be patient.

Lastly, despite everything I have said, *think of yourself first* and the child afterward. A happy, contented parent is a far better parent than one who is tense and frustrated; it has never failed to amaze me how the smallest improvement in a parent's emotional state can be reflected so quickly and so noticeably in his or her child. If a mother is happier and more contented, for instance, working in an office from nine to five while a competent nurse takes charge, than spending the day at home and hating it—then she should do so; her enjoyment of her baby during the early morning and evening hours will be far more genuine and wholehearted. If a mother works and slaves and runs herself ragged, she will eventually become one of those who make such bitter remarks to their teen-agers as, "Look at all the sacrifices I made for you." Such "sacrifices" are never appreciated and always provoke resentment rather than sympathy.

Of course I am not advocating a full-time job for every mother of a small baby. The decision should be strictly hers, based on both her own feelings and whatever financial or other family circumstances may apply. But whether she works outside the home full time, part time, or not at all, I do urge every mother—and father too—to look for ways to make the necessary chores involved in caring for a child as easy as possible. The less time and energy you spend on routine tasks, the more you can devote to the nonroutine activities that will make the real difference in your child's formative years: talking to him, reading to him, playing with him, cuddling him, getting to know and love each other.

That is what this book is all about.

I will have achieved my aim in writing it if, one day, when your great-aunt Martha comes to visit and sighs and shakes her head sadly at the sight of the myriad creases in little Susie's clean but unpressed dress, you can reply calmly and confidently as you and Susie turn the pages of a book together, "Who says it has to be ironed?"

Addendum

Unfortunately, there is not a single word in the English language that means "he or she." We do not like to refer to human beings as "it." On the other hand, constant repetition of "he or she" gets a bit boring. Nor do I wish to coin a new pronoun that will serve mainly to confuse the reader.

Consequently, you will find masculine pronouns in many instances where one sex or the other has not been specified. I beg the understanding and indulgence of the Women's Lib movement; no offense is meant. It is true, of course, that this is a traditional male chauvinist convention, since the majority of living human beings are, in fact, female. But, as it happens, the majority of human beings *born* are male—and by the age that serves as an upper dividing line for this book, males are still in the majority (that slight edge, by the way, is maintained through the mid-teens).

So that if a pronoun is to be favored here, "he" does, for once, in all fairness deserve the nod.

1

Feeding, in the First Place: He'll Eat When He's Hungry and Drink When He's Dry

Young parents I have known seem more concerned about the feeding of their children than about any other single aspect of child care. This concern begins to germinate, frequently, along about mid-pregnancy; it is nurtured by perusing such works as I have cited in the Introduction. It is also encouraged by articles by, and newspaper interviews with, nutritionists who surface, like the groundhog, from time to time—just long enough to view with alarm the malnourished state of our nation and to utter a series of dire predictions about the mental and physical prospects of the next generation.

The concern bursts into full flower the moment the baby comes home from the hospital. Sometimes it persists until the child leaves his parents' bed and board permanently. There have even been instances in which it has continued well beyond that point, branching out to envelop yet a third generation.

Worrying about what your child eats or does not eat will accomplish only one thing: it will make you a very nervous person. Infants and small children, as I have remarked, are very responsive to the emotional states of the adults around them. Thus, such worrying is likely to make your child a very nervous person too. Which is likely to affect his appetite and his digestion. It is a vicious cycle best avoided in the first place.

I cannot stress too strongly the fact—and it *is* a fact—that no normal child will either undereat or overeat if food is available to him on the one hand, and is not forced upon him on the other. The vast majority, including babies less than a month old, will let you know when they are hungry. Furthermore, an older child given a free choice of nutritious food (that is, not candy and such) will actually instinctively select a well-balanced diet! It may not be a diet that seems very exciting to you—but it will be a perfectly healthful one.

Later I'll have a bit more to say about eating habits when children reach that "real food" stage. At first, of course, the staple of an infant's diet is milk—mother's milk, cow's milk, or some other kind of formula your doctor may recommend —supplemented by whatever vitamins the doctor may suggest or prescribe. For those infants who cannot tolerate human milk or cow's milk—the latter is a not uncommon situation—the doctor will prescribe a substitute that is just as nutritious and filling. (Don't ever feed an infant—or an older child, for that matter—imitation milks, non-dairy "creamers" for coffee, and the like, as a substitute for milk or prescribed formula. Such products often contain excessive saturated fats and they do not provide sufficient vitamins, minerals, and other essential nutrients.)

How much milk? That depends on what he weighs. By and large, an infant needs about two to two and a half ounces of milk per pound during each twenty-four-hour period—which means that when your baby weighs, say, ten pounds he should be getting (and will drink, if it's offered) twenty to twenty-five ounces a day. Later, after other foods appear on his menu, he'll need less milk, since he'll be getting the same nutritional elements from other sources; by the time his diet is really varied, he'll need only about sixteen ounces (one pint, or half a quart) a day—and that, by the way, is all he'll *ever* need during his growing years, despite what you may hear from the dairy industry.

To the specifics. I think we might well begin with a comment on what has become, in some circles, one of the most overblown controversies of the century, and a subject to be avoided at social gatherings as carefully as religion and politics. To wit:

The Breast vs. the Bottle

Remember that there is no "right" way or "wrong" way to raise a child. This consoling maxim applies even to the most basic activity, providing your baby with nourishment. It is my firm conviction that the choice is up to each mother—despite the proselytizing and propaganda that may assault her from both sides.

The bottle-feeding advocates are by far the weaker of the two groups. There have been only a few articles in the press arguing, in the main, that breast feeding may instill deep feelings of jealousy in older siblings (there are apparently shades of Oedipus here). There is absolutely no reason why this should be so.

Chiefly, the Cassandras have been breast-feeding partisans, whose diatribes revolve around the "nature's way" theory: that human milk was meant for humans, cow's milk for calves, and any violation of this preordained scheme of things is likely to wreak havoc on both the soma and the psyche of the helpless infant. One well-known child-care guide—*the* well-known child-care guide, in fact, which was written in the mid-1940s—devotes a thirty-six-page chapter to breast feeding, a mere nineteen pages to bottle feeding.

Personally, I defy the most zealous champion of breast feeding as a superior method to pick out, from one hundred six-month-old babies, those who have been breast-fed and those who have been bottle-fed. But don't take my word for it. You should know that a study of over 1,500 infants was reported in 1971. The babies were divided into groups according to whether they were breast-fed, given cow's milk, or raised on other formulations, and were observed from birth until the age of one year; result: absolutely no differences in the growth and development of these children were detected. A similar 1972 study on a smaller group—with breast-fed and bottle-fed infants matched in factors such as socioeconomic level—produced like results. It is estimated, incidentally, that fewer than 20 percent of all American children are now breast-fed.

I am not arguing for either side. A mother who wishes to breast-feed her baby should receive encouragement from her doctor and her family. The mother who prefers to use the bottle should not feel that she is less maternal, that she is depriving her child, or that she is guilty of some nebulous sin. The baby, in short, will thrive either way—assuming that the mother is happy in her choice, and that her choice is her own and not that of her mother, her neighbors, her friends, or her doctor (unless, of course, there are special medical considerations that must be taken into account). In fact, since there are not in most instances any medical reasons for deciding one way or the other, the mother's feelings are paramount. It *has* been demonstrated that babies reared by parents who are resentful (at being forced into one or another sort of behavior, for instance)—which furor can easily fasten on the child—can experience retarded growth; such children can suffer from what is known as "deprivation dwarfism"—and the deprivation is emotional, not physical.

What I suggest you do, if you are a mother-to-be or new mother and you are in a quandary on this question, is: (1) determine your own feelings; (2) consider the relative advantages and disadvantages of each method vis-à-vis your own circumstances and life style. As follows.

Bottle feeding can, of course, be done by anyone—the baby's father, an older brother or sister, a baby-sitter—and thus offers more coming-and-going freedom for the mother. Your baby receives a standardized, dependable, nutritious formula—regardless of the mother's own state of health, and safely free of any medications she may take.

There are two disadvantages—one clear, one conceivable—to bottle feeding. One is, of course, that formula must be compounded, which is time-consuming, though not terribly. The other is that infant allergies to formula, while they do not occur with any great frequency, are not uncommon (formulas can easily be changed, though, after consultation with your pediatrician).

Breast feeding offers the distinct advantage that the milk is always available; no formulas have to be compounded. Mother's milk also offers a higher sugar content than cow's milk. Additionally, it contains antibodies that help the baby resist minor intestinal infections during his first few months (temporary resistance to *major* diseases was conveyed to him while he was in the womb).

There are also some advantages that accrue to the mother. Breast feeding helps the uterus shrink more quickly and also serves as a sort of contraceptive: the chances of becoming pregnant are greatly diminished while nursing (though they are not nil). And if a breast-fed baby spits up after feeding, the material will be odorless.

The major disadvantage is evident: the mother's freedom of movement is clearly restricted, since babies need to be fed much more often than adults find a meal necessary (although

an occasional bottle feeding, it should be noted, can be sub-
stituted for a breast feeding). And if you—or your friends
and neighbors—are embarrassed or offended by the sight of
a mother nursing her child, all the feeding must then be done
in private.

In short: make up your own mind.

Schedules (How Come He Says He's Hungry When the Clock Says He Isn't?)

People, as I shall remind you again in other connections,
are not clocks. You may have dinner religiously each evening
at six, seven, eight, or some other time. This is not because
you are regularly famished at that hour but because you have
found it convenient to gather the adults—or the adults and
older children—together at that particular time and partake
of nourishment. Actually, some of the folks at the table may
be famished, others may be somewhat hungry, and still others
could just as soon wait an hour or two. But the logistics of
setting separate tables to suit the digestive proclivities of
every family member are obviously impossible of attainment.

Babies, on the other hand, have not yet learned to regulate
their lives for over-all family convenience. While a baby born
in a hospital that does not provide for rooming-in is usually
brought out for feedings on a nice, neat four-hour schedule
(12-4-8, 9-1-5, or whatever the particular hospital uses), these
feedings do not necessarily coincide with the baby's actual
sensations of hunger. The mass feedings are of course necessary for the efficient functioning of the nursing staff; if they
were to feed every baby on demand, they would accomplish
little else. Nor will these clockwork feedings harm the child.

Once the baby is home, however, there is no reason not to
feed the baby whenever the baby's hungry, or at least closer
to those times than a hospital can possibly manage. I rec-

ommend what I call a *modified demand schedule*. Basically, the baby should be fed when he is hungry; but in line with my insistence that parents have their own lives to live (and that the child will eventually have to accommodate his desires to those of others anyway, and he may as well start now), and that parents need and deserve a night's sleep, he can be urged to take nourishment when he is not conscious of hunger.

I suggest that the baby be fed, by and large, whenever he is hungry—and just before the parents go to bed, whether he is hungry or not. Curiously, when most parents go to bed, the child is peacefully sleeping, yet it is probably nearly a hundred to one that within five minutes after the parents' retirement for the night the child will be issuing a call for sustenance. Do try to awaken your child before you go to bed—whether it's 9:00 P.M., 3:00 A.M., or any other hour—and see if he will take some milk. If he won't, you've lost only a few minutes; if he will, both parents can (hopefully) get a few hours of uninterrupted sleep.

Babies, incidentally, always get the right amount of sleep—for *them*. Only the parents—or only the mother, if she is breast-feeding—get deprived of needed sleep by frequent feedings. Bear in mind, too, that if the baby has long periods of sleep during the night he may very well eat more often during the day—possibly every two hours, or even every hour.

Keeping the child up during the day "to get him tired" rarely works, I'm afraid. Adults, who have learned to gear their instinctive physical actions and reactions to the demands of society, tend to forget that infants, not enjoying the benefit of society's proscriptions, can and do fall asleep anywhere, at any time, and in any position, if they are tired enough. They, unlike us, do not waste time worrying about hurting anyone's feelings by instantly seeking the sleep they want and need.

Breast Feeding: Notes for Novices

If you've decided to nurse your baby, be assured that there is every reason to expect the endeavor will be successful. After all, if the method didn't generally work, the human race would have died off with Eve. I never offer any advice to a mother who successfully nursed her first baby; she will instinctively make whatever adjustments are necessary with each succeeding child. I do, however, have a few things to point out to the mother breast-feeding her first child—in addition to the basics that are easy to pick up at prenatal classes (which I urge both prospective parents to attend).

When you begin to nurse, what will be released from your breasts will not be milk but a yellowish—and protein-rich—fluid called colostrum. The bluish-white milk will appear about the fourth day after delivery.

Be prepared for the fact that it may take a couple of weeks, or even a month or so, to strike a balance between the mother's milk supply and the baby's demands. Most babies can pretty easily empty a breast in five to seven minutes of active sucking. The mother needs rest in order for the milk to come in. If the baby sucks for forty-five minutes or an hour, with not much more than an hour's grace period between feedings, the mother will soon find herself worn to a frazzle and also worried that the baby is not getting enough milk. Contrary to old wives' tales, the milk supply at the beginning is diminished more by that exhaustion and anxiety than by too little nursing. Further, if the mother nurses too often or too long, particularly if she is of fair complexion and the baby is very vigorous, the nipples may become cracked, which makes nursing an agonizing experience rather than the delightful one it should be. (That problem, if it arises, should be discussed with your doctor.)

Until the nipples adapt to all this unaccustomed activity

—usually not more than a couple of weeks—it's a good idea to limit sucking time at each breast to ten minutes, or a total of twenty minutes in all, and nurse no more often than every two or three hours. If you feel that your baby's hungry in between, have your pediatrician or family doctor suggest an appropriate formula to offer for those feedings (don't just give the infant water; water is no substitute for nourishment).

Even if you have to give a bottle after each and every feeding, at first, don't be discouraged. Babies are remarkably adaptable; most can switch back and forth with no problem. Your baby will be getting the food he needs, the mother can relax and get some rest between breast feedings (fathers, remember, can offer bottles too, and usually enjoy it), and you will find that gradually the baby will take less and less from his bottle. After a while his needs and the mother's milk supply will equalize.

I urge that you do substitute an occasional bottle. That way, the baby will become accustomed to the idea. When the father comes home from work a bottle can be given by him while the mother sees to dinner—which will leave the child quiet and contented while the parents are enjoying a leisurely meal together. (By the next feeding, the mother is apt to have quite a healthy supply of milk, and hopefully the baby will sleep for a longer stretch and let Mother get five or six hours of uninterrupted sleep.) It is a good idea, too, for the parents to have an evening out once in a while, sans infant, and have the baby-sitter handle a bottle feeding; this tends to relax the mother and relieve tensions, which have been known to have an adverse effect on milk supply.

Just to underscore the supreme adaptability of infants— and their mothers—I might add that I have known a number of nursing mothers who have returned to full-time jobs within six weeks of their babies' births, nursing their infants only morning, evening, at night, and on weekends, while a

sitter or relative handled bottle feedings during the day. No
disaster has ensued: the mothers have continued to nurse for
six to twelve months; the babies have thrived; and there has
been a healthy, relaxed relationship between mother and
child.

The nursing mother should see to it that she gets a good,
balanced diet—including the equivalent of a quart of milk a
day; if the idea of drinking milk fills her with feelings of revul-
sion, she should ask the doctor to prescribe calcium pills, to
be taken with a specified amount of fluids, which will
perform the same function. (This, by the way, is not for the
baby but for the mother. If there is not enough of this element in her diet, milk manufacture will continue at the same
level—but the mother's own essential calcium supply will be
depleted.) Adequate rest is important too. Beyond that, just
don't worry about it; nothing seems to diminish the flow as
much as needless fretting. Milk, by the way, is milk, and one
mother's milk doesn't vary particularly in quality from any
other mother's. It's adequate quantity that's important. But
bear in mind that it may take a few weeks, and that women,
unlike Guernseys, are not sold for beef if they do not
promptly deliver an optimum milk supply.

Once you get past the first few weeks—believe me, it will
be smooth sailing from then on. You also will not have to
watch the clock; you'll know instinctively (yes, believe me,
you will) when the first breast is empty and it's time to offer
the second. Some babies are satisfied with only one at a single
feeding (next feeding, of course, you'll offer the other); some
want both each time. You will also know when the baby is
full: he stops sucking and contentedly drifts off to sleep.

When should a mother stop nursing? As with most aspects
of child raising, this is a very individual matter. I would say
that she should nurse as long as she wants to nurse and enjoys
it. There are some new mothers who try it once, in the hos-

pital, and find they really hate it—and that's that. Others continue until the baby is no longer interested in taking the breast—which can take place, roughly, anywhere from six months to two years. Most stop somewhere in between. It is solely the mother's decision and should not be commented upon by others; it is none of their concern. It will not hurt the baby—I reemphasize—if the mother stops breast feeding after two months, or five months, or one year, or some other period of time (or indeed does not breast-feed at all). It can, on the other hand, very *well* harm the child if he senses that what should be a nourishing experience, both physically and emotionally, is being offered him reluctantly, under duress.

When a nursing mother decides to wean her baby from the breast, the easiest and simplest step is to cut her fluid intake to a minimum and to nurse the baby only when she is uncomfortable, and only for as long as she is uncomfortable. There is no need for clock watching, for remembering which breast was given last, or any other tedium; her own discomfort will be perfectly obvious to her. Gradually the baby will nurse less and take the bottle more; drying up of the milk supply will take place within a week or so, without any need for pills, binders, or other tediums.

On Bottle Feeding, Including Some Things
Even Old Hands May Not Know

Most infants are started on a formula that consists, basically, of a combination of evaporated milk, water, and some form of sugar (or syrup). There are prepared products on the market, or you can compound your own formula according to your doctor's directions; your doctor is the best judge of what product should be chosen or what ingredients should go into your own formulation.

I am now about to dispel a couple of cherished myths.

One concerns sterilizing. I have yet to see a nursing mother boil her nipples or render them sterile any other way. A shower or bath each day is what most women, including nursing mothers, consider adequate cleanliness in our society, and I dare say the standards were a good deal lower before the advent of central heating and the broad availability of indoor plumbing—and are probably a good deal lower right now in some parts of our planet. Breast-fed infants do not seem to become ill because they ingest, along with their mothers' milk, some of the organisms that are present on all human skin—including their mothers' and their own.

It's probably a good idea to take some extra pains for the first couple of weeks—meaning that it's advisable to boil the water you use to mix the formula, and to go out of your way to use extremely hot tap water for washing bottles and nipples. *And* to make sure that you have good refrigeration—which is a continuing requirement for keeping any food, including a baby's formula, reasonably free of troublemaking bacteria. If you prepare formula as much as *twenty-four hours in advance*—whatever the baby's age—it is preferable to sterilize, since that's a long enough period for the accumulation of a significant number of bacteria.

The second myth concerns the temperature of what goes into an infant's stomach. When formulas were introduced for the feeding of newborn infants, around the beginning of the twentieth century, it was postulated—understandably—that, since mother's milk represented the ideal, every effort should be made to simulate it. In every particular. One of the things noted about that source of nourishment was that it issues forth, invariably, at body temperature—roughly 98.6° F. (37° C.), give or take a couple of degrees. It was therefore assumed that formulas should be heated to approximately that temperature, and for half a century parents and others who cared for infants spent anguished hours anxiously sprinkling drops of formula on their wrists in a frantic effort to pop the nipple in the baby's mouth just when the liquid had reached that "perfect" temperature. Of course the bottle had always been heated, so there was an inevitable cooling down/testing/more cooling/more testing period—during which both parent and famished infant grew more and more frantic and frustrated.

Thanks to a revolutionary study performed in the Premature Unit of Bellevue Hospital several years back, we now know there is no need to go through all these efforts and delays. Half the tiny babies in the study—by definition, underweight, delicate infants—were fed traditionally warmed formulas. The other half—also premature infants, no different from the control group—were fed ice-cold formulas, straight from the refrigerator. Both groups thrived; there was no significant difference in weight gain, cramps, spitting up, diarrhea, or any other results favorable or unfavorable. The only difference observed was that cold formula flowed a little more slowly through the nipple than warmed formula.

The medical world has finally figured out that the cold formula stays cold only about halfway through an infant's throat. By the time it reaches his stomach it has been sufficiently warmed by the heat of his own body so that it will not come as any sort of shock to his gastrointestinal tract. I urge you not to waste your time—and your child's—with such bothersome procedures as sterilization and bottle-heating. Be sure the bottles and nipples are clean, just as you are sure your own dishes and eating utensils are clean—and, I might add, thoroughly rinsed and free of soap or detergent residues. Be sure made-up formula is refrigerated, just as you keep other spoilable food refrigerated—and that your fridge is at the proper temperature for food keeping, meaning a maximum of 40° F. (4.4° C.), preferably 37° F. (2.8° C.). That's all. *Always look for the easy way.*

Formula, by the way, need not continue for very long. For years I have successfully placed infants of two months or ten pounds, whichever occurs earlier, on whole pasteurized milk. No boiling. No heating. No sterilizing. And ordinary water. (If it's not good enough to drink—would *you* be drinking it?)

So much for the myths. How much formula—or pasteurized milk, or whatever the baby is drinking at that point—do you offer in his bottle? I think it is a good idea to put in a little more than he is likely to take; remember that he will take precisely as much as he wants and, unlike adults, will not finish up every last drop in order to spare your feelings.

At the beginning, about three or four ounces is a good amount; chances are, he'll leave a little. When he drains the bottle, and is obviously looking for more—simply add to it. In other words, when a child begins to breeze through four ounces, start giving him a six-ounce bottle. Then proceed to eight ounces, or fill the bottle all the way to the top. The hole in the nipple should be small enough to give him about twenty minutes of sucking at each feeding.

There are some babies who, for reasons unknown to anyone, are what I call nibblers. They will take frequent, small amounts over a period of four to six hours: they wake up crying, they take a little bit, they nap contentedly for another hour or ninety minutes, then wake up hungry again. Often, you'll find they consume a rather enormous amount of milk over that four- to six-hour period—and that they will sleep for a good long stretch following the nibbling "binge." It is devoutly to be hoped that if your baby develops this habit he will do his nibbling during *your* waking hours and his extended sleeping during *your* sleep time. Some babies reverse things, and there is little you can do about it. Perhaps you will find it convenient to reverse your own schedule for a while—i.e., sleep during the daylight hours and prepare yourself to be relatively active at night. If that's not feasible, you might try nudging him toward your schedule by offering him more frequent feedings during the day, especially toward the end of the day. And keeping your fingers crossed. It is certainly a good idea to make nighttime feedings strictly business: save postfeeding "play times" for daytime feedings.

Next question, and one that new parents invariably ask timidly: how about propping a bottle? The timidity derives from the fact that a number of presumably authoritative writers have issued dire warnings about bottle propping, implying that the baby is liable—or even likely—to choke. The possibility exists, if the nipple is unusually fast-flowing because it has too large a hole; otherwise, there is not much likelihood of such a disaster. Most babies can turn their heads, and most of them can do so practically from the day they are born. (I mean that literally. Try putting your baby down on his stomach, without any effort on your part to turn his face in one direction or another. The odds are that he will not lie there with his little nose squashed into the mattress but will immediately turn his head to one side or the other.) To be on the safe side, I advise against bottle propping under the age of six months—but mainly for quite another reason.

Much of your baby's early impression of the world around him derives from his feeding experiences—not only the sustenance itself but the feeling of someone holding him and making contact with him, literally and otherwise. His earliest pleasurable experiences revolve around this dual sensation of being physically fed and of being, at the same time, held securely in someone's arms. It's really unfair to deprive an infant of these vital human contacts. Yes, there will be times when it's necessary, when something else has to be done and it cannot wait. But I urge you not to make a regular habit of bottle propping.

There is nothing wrong, by the way, in having someone

other than the mother or father feed the baby, including older siblings; they usually enjoy the experience thoroughly. Just be sure that the older child is comfortably and securely seated and knows how to hold both the baby and the bottle —including gradually increasing the tilt of the bottle as the baby drinks, so that the nipple stays full and the baby will swallow a minimum of air. If your young helper is younger than eight or ten, it's best to have the feeding going on where you can keep an eye on it.

When your baby is six or eight months old—or maybe three months or twelve months old; there's a good deal of variation—he will begin to get teeth. By that time you may have got into the habit of providing him with bottles of juice or milk during the night to nibble on as he sees fit since, if he's teething later rather than earlier, he may already be able to hold a bottle by himself.

One bottle of milk or juice at night will do no harm; it's usually drunk fairly rapidly. But for a child who demands several bottles during the night, make the second and subsequent bottles plain water. If you don't, and he sucks on a series of bottles of milk or juice every night, the lactic acid (in milk) or citric acid (in juice) will accumulate on his teeth, and you may eventually have a two-year-old with rotting baby teeth at the upper front of his mouth. If he initially resists plain water—resistance will be evidenced by quite audible protest—then, over a few days' time, dilute the milk or juice gradually, night by night; he will finally get accustomed to water. Of course a baby who drinks eight or ten bottles of water a night will be pretty soggy in the morning—but his teeth will be intact.

Another answer may be a pacifier, which we'll come to shortly. But not all babies will accept the substitute when they're used to a bottle in the crib at night—a bottle with real stuff coming out of it, not merely a disconnected nipple.

Is He a Good or Bad Burper, and If Not, Why?

Let me make one thing perfectly clear. *Some babies don't burp.* At *all.* Yet there seems, in my experience, to be some universal urge to extract a burp from all babies. And I have heard all sorts of moral judgments dispensed as a result of these efforts. Such as, "He's a good burper." Or, "He won't burp for me at all!" Or, "It takes him a long time to burp"—with the clear implication that he has willed it that way in order to annoy one parent or the other.

It will help if you understand what burping—in a baby—is. Most babies, in fact, do burp—but not, as I've pointed out, all babies. Most babies swallow some air from around the nipple—mother's or bottle's—with their milk or formula. The tighter the baby's grip on the nipple, the less air he'll swallow; a slack grip, conversely, will admit a great deal of air. We know that it is not a question of air inside a bottle: there is no air inside a breast, and yet breast-fed babies require burping no more and no less than bottle-fed babies.

There is not very much room in the small stomach of a baby. When air accumulates there, it is uncomfortable. Meaning: he needs to burp. At first, you will not know if your baby needs to burp or not, but there is an easy way to find out. As soon as he has finished his feeding, hold him upright against your shoulder or on your lap, and pat him on the back (some babies need to be burped once or twice during the feeding as well; you'll soon know if your baby is one of those).

Continue the back-patting for no more than one full minute. If nothing has happened, stop; if he needed to burp, he would have.

Sometimes the baby will have a fairly tight grip on the nipple, and the swallowed air bubbles are very small—so small that they cause no discomfort and do not need to be ejected immediately. You can pat such babies on the back for forty-five minutes and nothing will ensue except fatigue. About an hour later, the bubbles may coalesce into something large enough to burp up—and any milk sitting on top of the bubble may come up as well. This is a phenomenon called "spitting up" or "cheesing"; it is not vomiting and is not a symptom of illness. (If, on the other hand, a baby forcibly ejects the milk immediately after feeding—a phenomenon accurately described as "projectile vomiting"—that is something quite different; it may, in fact, be a serious condition, and the doctor should be called promptly if it occurs more than once; if you are unable to reach your own doctor, it is wise to take the child to the hospital.)

What is helpful is to try to figure out what type your child is—a non-burper, a grand-finale burper, or an intra-feeding burper. At the beginning, pull back on the bottle after the baby has consumed about an ounce—or release the breast after five minutes or so—and try to pull the nipple out of the infant's mouth. If he lets go, give him an opportunity to burp. If he seems reluctant to let go, don't force him; let him continue to suck, and give him another chance an ounce—or five minutes—later. Try this at one or two feedings, and you'll have an idea of what type of burper or non-burper your child may be.

That brings us to:

Pacifiers in the Scheme of Things, the Place of

There will be further comment on this subject in another chapter, in another context; right now, we are concerned with feeding phenomena.

Some babies need to suck more than is required merely to fill them with nourishing food. This is sort of an instinctive urge some babies have and others do not. Bear in mind—because it's relevant—that sucking is about the only active exercise very small babies get. Some like it more than others.

One way to deal with this, if you're bottle-feeding, is to get new nipples with smaller holes, so that the baby has to suck a little longer—and thus gets more fun from the whole procedure—to get the same amount of food. If you're nursing, offering just one breast at a feeding may provide him with the sustenance he wants at that point—he can empty one breast in five to seven minutes—plus a few minutes more of nonproductive sucking (if you don't mind being used as a pacifier). If neither of these ploys works, you may find that a pacifier is a virtual godsend. It will not, I assure you, hurt the child either mentally or physically.

Let us suppose, at this point, that you have provided the child with a pacifier—one of the little holeless nipples through which no sustenance whatever flows, but which can satisfy the sucking urge. (If you do not provide it, chances are he will suck his thumb, his fingers, his fist, or anything else available.) And that the baby wakes up crying. You ascertain that he is not wet, fevered, or in pain. You surmise that he has either a need for sustenance or a need to suck on his pacifier. The question is: which is it? The answer is simple: offer him one or the other (just make a wild guess; after all, you have a fifty-fifty chance of being right). If he grabs breast or bottle avidly, then spits it out after a few minutes, you will know he had the pacifier in mind. If you've offered the pacifier, and he spits that out and screams with annoyance, then what he wants is a nipple with milk coming out of it.

Just as infants can get hungry in the middle of the night, that old sucking impulse can come on them in the wee hours too. It is helpful to arrange things so your baby can lay hands on the pacifier quickly—i.e., before his questing cries have awakened the rest of the household. Some mothers scatter several pacifiers around the crib on the theory that he's bound to find one of them. Sometimes that works; sometimes it doesn't, and the baby spends a long—and noisy—time groping at one end of the crib, while all eight pacifiers have mysteriously found their way to the diagonally opposite corner. The best solution is probably the one thought up by a mother I know: she runs a rolled-up diaper through the ring on the pacifier, then safety-pins the diaper firmly to the sheet on each side of the pacifier, after positioning the pacifier conveniently for the baby. This avoids a lot of frustration for the baby, a lot of sleeplessness for the parents, and a lot of money spent on duplicate pacifiers. (This assumes that the baby stays in one position, which isn't always true; you may still have to get up—or have a duplicate.)

It should be emphasized that a pacifier is meant to function as a fulfillment of the sucking urge that cannot be satisfied by feeding (especially with the breast, in which the nipple hole cannot of course be made smaller)—*not* to serve as an around-the-clock tranquilizer. If your baby needs to suck during the night in order to fall asleep contentedly, fine. But if he acts cranky during his normal daytime waking hours it's better to distract him by providing some new stimulus—moving him from one room to another, playing with him, talking to him.

As soon as your baby has any teeth, check out the pacifier frequently, to see if there's any sign of disintegration. If so, replace it; when a pacifier's old and falling apart, there is always the possibility that small pieces could break off and cause him to choke.

2

Feeding, in the Second Place: "But, Doctor, He Doesn't Eat Anything at All!"

Sooner or later parents begin to have visions of their child, spindly and undernourished, going off to kindergarten with a lunchbox containing a bottle of milk and another of orange juice. Somewhere along the line, they reason, other foods must be introduced—solid foods, "real" foods. This anxiety may set in when the child is eight or nine weeks old—or even earlier—and the phrase I have often heard is that the baby "is eating *nothing* yet." When I ask how much milk he is taking in a twenty-four-hour period, I am told, "Oh, about thirty-five ounces."

Milk, some people tend to forget, is food; it is not served on a spoon, but it is food nonetheless. If a child is consuming thirty-five ounces of breast milk, whole pasteurized milk, or formula, he is getting well over 700 calories, plus substantial amounts of other food elements, essential minerals, and vitamins.

As with some other facets of child rearing, there are ever-present outside pressures, too, often related to what stage has been reached by an infant down the block who is just a few weeks older than yours. Parents of first babies, in particular, are sometimes anxious to start their children on solid foods—occasionally as early as two weeks of age. I urge you to resist these pressures. There is good reason to wait a little while. Several reasons, in fact.

Sucking is instinctive, something a baby is born with. Swallowing semisolid material is not. His jaws and throat muscles need time to develop strength; it makes sense to begin building up that strength with liquids rather than sirloin steak. Nor is an infant's digestive system instantly prepared to cope with the complexities of other foods. And, thirdly, the emotional and physical sense of security the child derives from breast or bottle feeding should be firmly established before he is placed in the less personal situation of someone's feeding him from a spoon.

Although some doctors may start a baby on solids as early as the age of two months, while others will wait until five months, I usually recommend—assuming I feel the baby's size and development are adequate—fourteen to sixteen weeks as a good time, i.e., between three and four months. You begin, of course, with puréed foods; generally the two that are started first are fruits and cereals. I usually suggest starting with fruit, because it tastes good and most babies like it.

You can purée your own cooked fruits in your blender— but the packaged baby cereals have an advantage over other types, in that they are fortified with iron. By the age of four to six months, your baby does need to start getting some iron; prior to that time, he's been depending on iron that was stored in his liver during the prenatal period. (Insufficient iron can result in anemia. If your baby is more than six months old and has taken, essentially, nothing but milk, you should schedule a prompt consultation with your doctor.) Many babies don't like cereal. A good way to get around that initial distaste is to mix it with something else—with fruit, with formula, with milk.

Bear in mind, when you first present solid food—cereal, fruit, or whatever your own doctor may suggest—that your baby is accustomed to taking his nourishment from a nipple; I do not think it is quite fair to assault a famished child with an out-of-the-blue offering of a strange new food on a strange new implement. Give him some milk first—say, about half what you would have given at an average, no-solids feeding. Then offer the spoon; use a special "baby" spoon if you like, but you'll find the little demitasse (espresso) spoons are a very convenient size and hold a good mouthful for an infant who's just starting to take solids.

Shove the spoon gently but firmly well into the baby's mouth, far enough back so that he's bound to swallow the food. (If you place the spoon at the tip of his tongue, his reflexive action will be to reject it—i.e., spit it out.) He may take hardly any at first, or he may take quite a lot. Be patient, and keep trying at each feeding. Try until (a) the baby absolutely refuses to take any more, or (b) the jar or dish is empty, or (c) your hand gets too tired to continue—whichever happens first. Then finish the feeding with more milk, offering either the rest of the bottle or, if you're nursing, the other breast.

Let us suppose that after a week or two of this your baby is taking and enjoying solid foods—so much that he refuses to take more than the tiniest quantity of milk. Do not panic. There are many foods that are rich in calcium; you can supply the equivalent in the form of soft cheese, ice cream, custard, pudding, yoghurt. If the baby doesn't like any of these things either, you can do one of two things. You can sneak the equivalent of a pint of whole milk into his solids in the form of powdered milk; or you can discuss with your doctor the advisability of adding a calcium supplement to his diet.

In general—and this applies later on, as well—I don't think it's a good idea to add chocolate to milk. That ploy can lead the child to expect sweeteners in any food he doesn't care for. It can also lead, eventually, to huge dental bills.

What do you do if the problem is precisely the reverse—if your baby is approaching the age of five or six months and absolutely disdains all solids? Don't despair. Try cutting his milk ration down to twenty-four ounces per twenty-four hours (you can do this without changing liquid intake or sucking time by giving him forty-eight ounces of liquid that is actually twenty-four ounces of milk diluted with an equal amount of water). This will not provide enough calories and the child will be hungry. If you offer a variety of tasty solids several times a day, even the most stubborn infant will begin to eat some after a few days. But do be patient—and don't get angry; if you do, you'll only make both yourself and the baby miserable. Eventually, you will find one or two foods he seems to like—or at least rejects less strenuously than others. Stick with those for a while, then gradually offer him more variety.

By about four or five months of age, many infants are too heavy for the average infant seat. But most of them can at that point be propped up in a chair, even if they can't yet sit unsupported. Do so by putting a pillow between the baby's back and the back of the chair—high chair or low chair, whatever you prefer—and tying something around him, secured to the back of the chair, so he won't topple forward.

Now, with the baby upright, you can try introducing a bottle with a straw—not a regular soda-pop straw but a special (and inexpensive) type made for baby bottles; he'll probably be unable to hold the bottle all by himself, but he's ready to try, and as time goes by he'll become more adept at it. When he learns to drink sitting up, he will be less likely to demand a bottle at night when he goes to bed.

By this time, too, the baby's digestive apparatus is sufficiently developed that you can rapidly expand his menu—in flavor, if not in form. Foods must still be pretty mushy at this stage; there's the matter of teeth, and most babies at this age have few if any. But there is no reason why he cannot enjoy just about anything the rest of the family eats, so long as the consistency is adapted to his needs. You need not prepare anything special; just make good use of your leftovers! It's easy, if you have a blender and a good freezer—one that stays at a dependable 0° F. (−18° C.).

When you're clearing dishes from the dinner table, and family members don't seem inclined to finish every last scrap, and there's not enough to go around for another meal (what, after all, does one do with one slice of beef, eight peas, and three forkfuls of mashed potatoes?), simply whisk it away, dump it all into a container, refrigerate it, and save it for blending for the baby. Save unused gravy, too, as well as meat juices and pot liquors (liquids in which vegetables have been cooked—which contain many nutrients). Then, a couple of times a week, toss an appropriate mixture in the blender, using the liquids to bring the mixture to proper blending consistency. You can combine things that weren't served together, even; nothing wrong with mixing steak and chicken (veal and apple pie, though, strikes me as rather unfair). Blend, then pour the result into an ice-cube tray and slide it into your freezer. When it's solidly frozen, extract the cubes, put them into a plastic bag, label it with date and contents, and toss it back in the freezer.

Frozen leftovers keep for four to six months—so now you have a steady source of instant meals for the baby. When you're at a loss, simply take out a few cubes, thaw and warm them; voilà, dinner! This is a very economical system. It also avoids such things as compulsive plate emptying and the forcing of foods on other family members—things that can lead to resentments, arguments, and frequently overweight. Additionally, it accustoms the baby to parental cooking; which is highly desirable, and the sooner the better, since he is going to eat at the family table eventually.

At some point along the line—often, at about a year, perhaps a bit later—your baby will enter the hand-to-mouth phase. You will observe him picking things up and putting them to, or in, his mouth. Usually these are not edible things. But since he's familiar with the motion, why not make the object in his hand something nourishing, and see what he does with it? Use things that are soft enough for him to nibble or gum off small pieces, large enough so the object can't be swallowed whole. You might start, for example, with a cracker; a piece of semisoft cheese; a cooked carrot, or stalk of asparagus, or broccoli spear; a slice of liverwurst; a handful of hamburger. *Never* turn your back on the child during such experiments; if he does bite off more than he can handle, and starts to choke, you want to be able to leap forward instantly and get the lump out of his throat. (Done by reaching in and grabbing it with your fingers, or by holding him upside down by the heels and clapping him on the back so he'll cough it up.)

Spoon-feeding himself is quite another matter. You may be able to persuade your baby to try it at about fourteen months. On the other hand, you may not. The baby who handles a spoon efficiently at a year and a half is pretty unusual; with most children, it won't occur until around the age of two. Do, as with all the prior procedures, have patience and encourage the youngster to learn. If you are so concerned about getting the food into the baby that you become exasperated with his fumbling and pick up the spoon yourself, he will make little progress; he'll be content to pick up his bottle and let you continue to run the spoon-feeding department. If your youngster is reluctant to try, I suggest an approach similar to that for the child who earlier clings to milk and balks at solids: in short, a little deprivation. Sit him down in front of foods you know he likes and that you believe he's physically capable of managing with a spoon. Do so repeatedly. And don't let him have so much milk—or juice either, for that matter—that he'll fill up on it and not have any appetite for (i.e., incentive to try) anything else.

Self-feeding can be a terrible mess; a great deal of the food may land everywhere except the baby's mouth. But it's worth the effort because the baby generally enjoys it and, mainly, because he's got to learn sometime, and it may as well be earlier rather than later. (And if you're planning another child before long, it will be nice if this one can feed himself by the time the second arrives.) Bear in mind that a small child's attention span is fairly short. It's best, at the start, to concentrate on foods containing iron, the one element missing from milk and juice—that is, meats, dark green vegetables, eggs, whole-grain breads.

There is one problem I may as well mention; it's fairly common, and by no means alarming or abnormal. That is the baby who—although he may even have a full set of teeth—simply doesn't like lumps of any kind and will spit out anything with real substance to it, no matter how small you cut it up. This may persist until the age of two or even three. If you try to force little pieces of meat, vegetables, etc., on him, you will end up spending half the day on your knees mopping up the floor. It's easier to continue such a child on puréed foods, gradually offering such things as cooked carrots that he will discover he can turn to mush in his mouth if he wants to. Eventually he'll come around.

Getting off the Bottle

I find that most babies will start showing interest in a cup, and drinking therefrom, on some occasion when they happen to notice someone else drinking from a cup or glass. This might happen any time after the age of six months. The child observes, for example, a parent drinking juice from a glass. He extends his hand; this means he is curious. Put it to his lips and see what happens. Chances are that most of the liquid will run down his face and very little will find its way into his mouth. He is obviously not ready to cope with a cup yet. But he *is* ready to start learning.

Begin by giving him small amounts of liquid in a little plastic cup. At first, of course, you'll have to hold the cup for him; later he'll begin to grasp it himself. It's a good idea, by the way, to start with juice rather than milk, because you'll probably run into less resistance. Most babies continue for a while to need the sucking experience—whether from breast or bottle—and will want to get the better part of their milk, if not all of it, from the nipple; milk, they apparently reason, is supposed to come out of nipples and does not properly belong in a cup. If the baby will take any milk at all from a cup by the time he's a year old, he's considerably more advanced than most.

When can you look forward to your child's being completely weaned from the bottle? That depends entirely on the individual youngster, and it can be quite variable. Some babies will happily surrender the bottle as soon as they can manage the cup. Some babies seem to have a stronger sucking need than others do; there are even dedicated suckers who, while they take some milk from a cup, insist upon clinging to the bottle until the age of two or three years. There is of course a strong security factor here, and I think it is cruel to arbitrarily whip the bottle away from a child before he is old enough to understand it. I do advise stopping the bottle at three, if you haven't persuaded the child to let it go before that; a child this age is verbal enough to understand, if the situation is explained to him, and compensatory emotional experiences can be offered. If the bottle is removed forceably before that stage, the child will of course get used to the new situation—but he will go through a good deal of anger and frustration before he does, and he is likely to start sucking on everything in sight, as well; I don't think it's worth it.

Even at three, I would not take the bottle away if, at that point, there's an imminent upheaval in the family—a move to a new home, the arrival of a new baby, a divorce, what have you; you cannot inflict so many elements of insecurity upon a child all at once. It is better to let the child keep the bottle until that particular crisis is over.

Chacun à Son Goût, Maybe, But He Sure Does Eat Funny

Let us say that your child is now two—or two and a half, or three—years old, is taking his drink from a cup and his food from a spoon, and has sampled most of your usual family menu. No more problems, right? He'll be eating "normally," like everyone else, from now on, right? Yes and no. No, he is not likely to assume adult eating habits in the near future. But "problems" will ensue only *if you create them*.

Children from the age of about a year until around five are not very big eaters. Rarely will they consume more than one decent meal a day—decent by your standards, that is. The rest of the day they will tend to nibble. Many children will prefer to eat small amounts—more than snacks, but certainly less than full meals—four or five or six times a day. And it may not seem to you that the child is getting an adequate, much less nutritious, diet.

I commented at the beginning of the first chapter that no child will deliberately undereat. If there is food available, he will eat. If there are assorted foods available, he will eventually choose those that provide a nutritionally balanced diet. Remember that milk is a nearly complete food. A youngster who demands a constant diet of, say, ice cream garnished with raisins and raw green peppers may have peculiar tastes from your point of view (and mine), but nutritionally he'll be fine: raisins are a fine source of iron, and green peppers are chock-full of vitamin C (unless they're cooked, in which case the vitamin is left in the cooking liquid for the most part).

I do not suggest, of course, that you deliberately offer such weird dishes. Simply that you make an assortment of nourishing foods—fruits, vegetables, cereals, meats, fish, poultry, eggs, and so on—available, and that you do not spend time worrying about what your child chooses to eat or leave. And, most emphatically, that you do not go out of your way to prepare special dishes for a preschooler.

Young children not only have small—and often inconsistent—appetites but are highly reluctant to experiment with new or strange foods. If you have prepared an exotic new dish for the entire family, by all means offer three-year-old Michael a taste. But unless you have very thick skin—and unlimited time and money—do not create a special dish just for Michael's lunch, even a *non*-exotic one. If you go to the trouble of broiling him a lamb chop, and he then decides he does not want to eat it—or does not want to eat anything at all at that time—it will be very difficult for you to keep your temper. You have bought the chop, gone to the trouble of cooking it, soiled a pan and a plate which you will have to wash, and what are you going to do with it now? I urge you to make any food preparation done just for the child as easy and inexpensive as possible; if he refuses a slice of cheese, a piece of bologna, or a peanut butter and jelly sandwich, no food, and little time, will have been wasted, you will not feel like kicking yourself for going to all that trouble, and you can cheerfully say, "Okay, maybe later. Shall we go out to play now?"

By the same token, it is a great mistake—as many a rueful parent has discovered—to give a child, even if he *is* hungry, an indefinite choice. An imaginative youngster, when asked,

"What would you like for supper?" may very well respond with, "Pheasant under glass." Your "Seriously, now," may lead to an infinite series of more realistic but no more workable responses, such as, "Strawberry ice cream!" (the last of what you had in the freezer was finished the day before) or "Pizza pie like we had last week!" (consumed at an Italian lunchroom, the nearest of which is fifty miles distant). You will find it far more efficient, and less wearing, to offer him a flat choice of two things: "Would you like to have a ham sandwich or a cheese sandwich?"—and then give him whichever he chooses. If he chooses not to finish it, okay; it can be saved for another time. And children often like to do their eating on the run rather than at formal, sit-down "meals."

As for what you provide in the way of snacks, I do feel that for various reasons certain things should be excluded. Potato chips, pretzels, and the like, for instance, have little food value and will simply fill a child up so that he'll have no room or desire to avail himself of more nutritious foods.

Candy and cake are similarly undesirable, and offer the added prospect of dental damage. If you explain to a child (if and when he raises the question) that you do not want him to have lollipops because they are bad for his teeth, chances are he will accept this because it is logical, and will even remember it when he finds himself in other situations, as in someone else's home; I have heard two-year-olds say matter-of-factly to well-meaning folk who have offered such goodies, "No, thank you, my mommy and daddy won't let me have one." Children can survive quite well without candy and cake.

It isn't really fair, I must admit, to make the rule such a hard-and-fast one that the child is totally excluded from group activities. Susie is going to feel pretty left out if she goes off to a fellow four-year-old's birthday party with such parting instructions as, "Now I don't want you to eat any of the cake, and I don't want you to eat any of the candy; it's all right to have a little ice cream, but that's all." It is probably better to get the idea across to Susie that such sweets are festive foods limited to special occasions and are not to be eaten as a regular thing.

Another kind of snack that's inadvisable for children of preschool age is popcorn, nuts, and things containing whole nuts—these, from a safety viewpoint. They can be easily—very easily—aspirated, that is, drawn into a child's windpipe, an event that poses the very real risk of asphyxiation. An adult can also swallow a nut "the wrong way"—but adults, and older children, have larger (thus, less readily blocked) windpipes, as well as far better cough reflexes, and can bring up a nut or hunk of popcorn more easily.

For the same reason, it is well to remove the pits from fruits—which are of course perfectly fine snacks—until you're quite sure your youngster knows just how to eat around pits; the larger the pit—e.g., a peach pit—the greater the danger. If a youngster does swallow a small pit, such as a prune pit—that is, if it does not choke him but actually gets swallowed—nothing will happen. The narrowest part of the gut is up in the neck. If the pit gets past that part, it will just keep going and eventually emerge from the other end; there is no record of anyone's growing a plum tree in his gastrointestinal tract. Tough-skinned fruits, such as apples, should be peeled for children of this age, since it's difficult for them to chew the skin properly. By and large, as a general rule—so you won't have to stop and consider each fruit—it's probably a good idea to pit and peel all fruit for a small child, except where the pits are clearly minuscule (e.g., grapes) or the fruit is likely to fall apart if its thin skin is removed (e.g., plums).

Aside from fruits (and fruit juices), there are plenty of other safe and healthful snacks you can make available without resorting to candy, chips, or nuts. Raisins, for one thing. Peanut butter, for another. Also cold cuts, cheese, raw vegetables, leftover meat and poultry.

Preschoolers generally have horrendous table manners. For that reason, as well as their unpredictable appetites, many parents prefer to feed a small child on his own, rather than at the regular family table. It's entirely up to you. If you do invite your three- or four-year-old to partake of meals with the rest of the family, I think it is important to then treat the child *like* the rest of the family. By this I mean that table conversation should not center around one individual's tastes or eating habits.

Mealtime should be a pleasant situation for everyone, not only for emotional reasons but from a physical viewpoint as well: tension and anger can seriously interfere with proper digestion. Who has eaten what, and how and why, does not make good table conversation; I think the only appropriate comment on the food being served is along the lines of, "My, isn't this delicious!" If little Michael does not happen to care for something that has been served to him, there is no reason to make a public announcement of the fact; he should simply refrain from eating it.

Nor should a parent initiate a discussion of what Michael has eaten or not eaten. After the meal is over, you might quietly comment, "I see you didn't eat your asparagus." He may then indicate that he does not like asparagus, or that he did not care for the sauce, or that after he had finished his chicken he simply was no longer hungry. This will give you some guidelines about what—and how much—to serve him in future.

I might add that, in my view, nothing is more boring than to dine with folks who spend the entire meal discussing the relative merits or demerits of this or that dish. People who start doing this in childhood often continue it into adulthood; they are generally not popular dinner companions.

Very few children like cooked vegetables. It is true that there are essential nutrients in cooked vegetables. But the same food values are available in fruit, which most youngsters do like. You may also find that a preschooler who shuns vegetables in the usual form served at meals is delighted to eat the same foods raw. If a child prefers his cauliflower, or string beans, or peas, or peppers, or mushrooms, or carrots raw, why argue with him? He likes them that way, they may be even more nutritious (vitamin C, for one, gets cooked out), and preparation is a whole lot easier. Let him eat them raw.

A perennial question related to this whole problem is whether a child should be denied dessert if he has not finished his main course. Personally, I don't think so. Dessert, ideally, should be something that is nutritious as well as tasty—fruit, for example, or ice cream. I don't feel that one food should be used as a threat vis-à-vis another, as in, "Finish your broccoli, or you won't get your ice cream." Both are foods; both are nourishing. If the threatening approach is used, the child is likely to infer that broccoli is some sort of medicine and ice cream has merits far beyond those of other foods. This is a distortion. (I shall comment, further on, about the whole practice of imputing moral or emotional significance to foods and the eating thereof.)

Each family, of course, sets its own house rules about meals. Some parents may feel that a child should at least sample everything that is served, while not insisting he eat a full portion of something he does not care for. Others will simply not serve that particular food to the child, while still others will provide a substitute that the child does like. How you run your household is, of course, up to you. But I do urge that you be consistent about it. And that you realize that everyone's appetites may vary from time to time. The idea of forcing a child—or anyone else—to finish everything on his plate strikes me as extremely unfair, since you may have put too much on his plate in the first place.

Whatever your feelings on the foregoing, there are three

rules that should be followed from a health and safety viewpoint:

1. When meat or other foods need to be cut, a parent should do the cutting. No preschooler should handle a knife, at the table or any other time.

2. Small bones are in the same category as nuts and popcorn: they can be accidentally swallowed, not only choking the youngster but, because they are sharp, doing real damage to his throat or gut as well. A steak bone or a chicken or turkey leg is fine; a child can simply nibble the meat from it. But smaller and softer bones—those of chicken wings, for example—can be easily bitten through, and fragments swallowed or aspirated. Fish, for the same reason, should be thoroughly boned before you serve it to a child.

3. Do not permit the child, or anyone else, to talk with his mouth full of food. The social aspects of this practice are not very important. What is important is that if one talks, or laughs, with a mouthful of food (or drink), it can be easily aspirated. As you must know from reading the newspapers, people—including grownups—have been fatally choked that way. Anyone with food in his mouth should keep his mouth closed, chew the food thoroughly, and swallow it, before speaking. And if someone is about to tell a hilarious story, let the rest of the family finish whatever they have in their mouths before the joke is told. I can tell you that once I very nearly drowned on a mouthful of coffee when a punch line came sooner than I had expected; no one is immune to this kind of mishap.

This Must Be Love, Because He Ate So Well

There are two phrases I hear from parents from time to time that truly infuriate me. Both attribute moral and emotional significance to eating.

One, addressed to a child, is "Eat, like a good boy (or girl)." If this meant, "Eat as a good boy does; try not to spill your milk, do not drop your mashed potatoes on the floor, and chew your food properly," it would be fine. But that is not usually the implication. Usually the clear suggestion is that eating, per se, is a demonstration of desirable behavior —and that failure to eat (whether because of lack of appetite or any other reason) is not socially acceptable. You can see, I trust, where this might eventually lead.

The second dangerous idea voiced by parents is frequently phrased this way: "Doctor, he won't eat for me." At home, it becomes, "Eat for Mommy, dear," or "Come on, let's see you finish your cereal for Daddy." If the child is eating as a favor to a particular individual, it follows logically that (a) he need not eat in that individual's absence; (b) refusing to eat is a good way to express anger or annoyance with that individual; and (c) the more he eats, the more firmly he will implant himself in that person's good graces, and the more love and affection he will enjoy.

People who are led to believe, in childhood, that eating is a form of earning love, friendship, and social acceptability tend to grow up with some rather peculiar notions about this basic function. These are the people who are inclined to use food as a substitute for pleasant human intercourse and as an antidote for frustrations and disappointments. They tend to obesity, and generally are not very happy or healthy human beings.

There is one reason, and only one, for eating: to fuel one's body. I urge you to be sure that your child does not get any other ideas about it.

3

"I Think I Have to Go, But Maybe I Don't": The Trials of Toilet Training

The time to start giving thought to this subject is, believe it or not, the day you bring your first baby home from the hospital. At that point, of course, the actual "training" period is blessedly distant. But, now and later, life will be far less traumatic for both parent and child if you remember that:

1. Elimination is a perfectly normal and necessary physical process. You will have to assist your child with this process until he is old enough to handle it by himself. It may be a bit of a nuisance but it will help if you get used to it, treat it as a routine matter, and banish any initial feelings of "disgust."

2. There are no ethical values associated with this process. Baby nurses in hospitals are fond of delivering such ponderous moral judgments as, "He had a good stool"—often, curiously, in a tone that implies the presumably praiseworthy material was the result of a collaborative effort. Stools may be many things—soft or firm, light or dark, frequent or infrequent—but they are neither virtuous nor evil.

Broadly speaking, the sequence of events falls into three fairly distinct stages. It would be well to keep the two cardinal principles firmly in mind through them all.

Stage 1: Strictly Diapers

By this I mean the time between the day of your baby's birth and the day he decides to advance to Stage 2. You will notice that I am not being very explicit. That is because no parent—and no pediatrician, either—can possibly know just how long it will last. It is the period during which you have no reason to entertain any realistic hope that your infant will abandon diapers in the immediate future. It is also the period during which your friends and relatives will generally refrain from pointed remarks concerning your baby's progress or lack of it (if this does not seem to be true, either you are nearing Stage 2 or you have an unusually large-for-his-age child and you will find some pertinent pointers in the Introduction).

Your Stage 1 responsibilities revolve around (a) the mechanics and (b) developing an awareness of what is normal and what is not, so that medical care can be sought if it's needed.

Most parents, I find, are concerned from the start—sometimes before the start—about diapers. You do have a choice. You can purchase and launder diapers yourself. You can use a diaper service, which takes away dirty diapers and supplies you with clean ones periodically. Or you can use disposable diapers. (For comment on quantity, see page 89.)

There is, by the way, a safety feature with disposable diapers: you need not use pins. Ordinary cellophane tape (Scotch, Tuck, etc.) works fine. Of course you have to discard the tape with the diaper, which means a little extra expense—but you'll be sure your baby will never swallow a safety pin, and neither you nor he will be stuck by one. Some disposable diapers, in fact, are now being made with adhesive closures.

Either a diaper service or disposable diapers will, of course, save you the burden of doing the washing yourself, and either is thus a time- and effort-saving option if you can afford it; after the age of about two months, the costs tend to be about the same, in my experience (you might do some comparison shopping in your own community). The do-it-yourself way is cheaper but takes more of your time and effort. Those are really the sole criteria; I have found no difference, among the three systems, in the physical or psychological health of babies, or in the occurrence of diaper rash.

In good conscience, that last statement should be slightly qualified. I do make a point, to parents, of the importance of proper laundering; improper laundering *can* cause—or further irritate—diaper rash. Diaper services can generally be depended upon to know what they are doing. If you wash diapers yourself, it's best to soak them in a borax solution (a teaspoonful to a gallon of water) before washing; wash them with a *mild soap*; and rinse them very thoroughly—in plain water, not in any special chemicals.

A second early concern is frequently, "How often should I change his diapers?" The answer depends a good deal on your baby, and that answer will come to you before many weeks have gone by. In short, there is no rule whatever. Small babies can have anywhere from one stool every three days to twelve bowel movements a day. Frequency of urination is even more variable. It is really much easier to change a diaper at *your* convenience than to try to whisk away the results of every elimination episode; if it upsets the baby to lie around with a damp diaper, change it—but if not, why bother? He's probably going to wet again very soon anyway.

A frequent question involves the use of waterproof panties. This happens to be a good question, and there are two sides to it.

One side is the obvious advantage, particularly with a child who is old enough to get around and onto the furniture —including other people's furniture—and assorted laps. Waterproof pants can prevent a great deal of extra laundry and dry cleaning in your house, and embarrassment in other people's houses.

The other side is that these pants do, in fact, encourage diaper rash, precisely because they keep the moisture in—and on the child's skin. There is an ingredient in urine called urea; in the confines of waterproof panties, bacteria act on this substance to produce ammonia, which is highly irritating. The child's skin is further irritated by bacteria in feces, by blocking of the sweat ducts, and by mere rubbing against the damp diapers.

There is no simple answer. You do not want to cause your child discomfort or pain. Nor do you want to be faced with urine stains—and worse—all over your living-room furniture and clothing and that of your friends. I think the best solution is to use the plastic panties when it's necessary—when the child is out of crib or playpen—and avoid them when it isn't. If your youngster has a tendency to diaper rash (some children seem to be more susceptible than others), yet is mobile enough to need this protection, you might make an effort to change him more frequently when he's wearing the waterproof panties.

The appearance—color and consistency—of an infant's urine is not markedly different from that of an adult, with one exception. Do not be alarmed if you occasionally find *pink stains* on your baby's diapers—a pale pink, distinctly unlike the red or brownish hue of bloodstains. The pink does not appear in the urine itself but results from chemical reactions in urate crystals when diapers have been damp for a period of time. It is, as I said, nothing to be concerned about. Do, however, call to your doctor's attention any other oddities you may note in your baby's urine—in color, consistency, or odor—or any pain or discomfort the child seems to suffer when he urinates.

You should also note, at the earliest opportunity, *how* your new baby urinates. With a boy, the criteria are fairly clearcut: he should be able to produce a two- to three-foot stream if nothing is in his way (if you've ever been sprayed in the eye during changing or bathing, that settles that question); the stream a girl shoots out is of course considerably smaller. The important point, with either sex, is that voiding should be initiated abruptly, continue with gradually diminishing force, then stop fairly suddenly (with perhaps a small trickle at the end). Alert your doctor if your baby seems to urinate in trickles; it may mean there is some stricture in the passage, which can and should be corrected—since, uncorrected, it could lead to serious infections and other ills of the urinary tract and kidneys. And if your baby boy produces a stream— of whatever length—that seems to be unusually thin, as if it has been squirted through a pinhole, that too is something your doctor should know; it could mean the opening at the end of the penis needs to be made a little larger—which can easily be done, and prevents any future problems.

As far as stools are concerned, there is a good deal more latitude in what constitutes normalcy. And what is normal for an infant is a far cry from what most of us would consider normal in an adult or an older child.

Take frequency. The number of times your baby's bowels move each day is likely to astound you. A perfectly normal, healthy baby may produce as many as ten or twelve stools within a twenty-four-hour period. The average, though, is three or four.

A word about averages. Averages of whatever sort are arrived at by taking a fairly large group of whatever you are averaging and adding up values and dividing by the number of units in order to arrive at a "mean." Or, by arranging your group in order—of height, weight, yearly earnings, number of bowel movements per day, or whatever—and then pinpointing that individual who falls precisely in the middle; this provides another kind of average, called a "median." It would probably be best if we all avoided mentioning averages. Many people, confronted with an average, are seized with an irresistible compulsion to compare themselves or their behavior (or their children's) with it, and to fret if they fail to correspond. Averages can, however, provide sometimes useful guidelines—if one views them in perspective and remembers that they *are* merely averages. And that while "average" is usually "normal"—normal is by no means necessarily average.

Back to your baby's bowel movements. As the child grows, the frequency will—I am sure you will be happy to hear—decrease, until eventually an individual pattern is established. You will note that I have not specified "once a day" or any other rigid regimen. Purveyors of over-the-counter cathartics are fond of lauding a vaguely defined condition called "regularity," with the implication that any departures from that condition are somehow "bad." "Regularity," to your grandmother—and possibly to your parents as well—meant "every day, once a day." Like clockwork. Some members of the older generation have chronic diarrhea (they call it "constipation") because they live on laxatives.

People, young or old, are not clocks. A perfectly normal pattern for one individual's bowel movements may indeed be once a day—but for another individual, an equally normal pattern may be three times a day, or once every two or three days. Nor should occasional slight departures from those patterns cause you undue concern. *Distinct, continuing*, or *frequent* departures do mean the doctor should be called—unless there is a clear reason for the departure; as we shall see, certain events in your baby's life (including the addition of new foods to his menu) are bound to cause a change in his stools—notably in color and consistency, sometimes in frequency as well.

In short, become familiar, generally, with your own child's usual or normal pattern—the pattern that is normal for him, not necessarily for anyone else. And if there is a deviation from that pattern, for which there are no obvious reasons, report it to your doctor.

Which brings us to the question of the appearance of your baby's stools. If you are like most first-time parents I have known, you have probably assumed your baby's stools will resemble your own stools, more or less. You are in for quite a surprise.

The very first movements of a newborn baby do not produce proper stools at all. What is excreted during the first two or three days after birth is something called meconium—a greenish-black material that consists of bile, mucus, and other wastes accumulated in his intestines while he was in the womb.

By the time he comes home from the hospital the appearance of his stools generally shifts to some extent toward what you would regard as "normal." But just as with frequency, there is a tremendous variation in "normal" from one baby to another—and even within the same baby from one day to the next and one movement to the next.

Very young babies often have rather loose, greenish stools. This is because what they eat goes through their little guts fairly quickly, and the bile secreted by the liver into the intestines will not have had much of a chance to change to other products that are yellower or browner in color. Further, young babies do not yet secrete bile in a nice, regular fashion, as older folks do. Thus, some stools may contain practically none at all and will be quite light in color—while others, depending upon both the quantity of bile and the chemical changes that may or may not have taken place, will vary from green to dark olive to definitely brown. Gradually, as your baby's diet changes and solid foods are added, his stools' color and consistency will begin to approach that of adults.

With this apparent all-over-the-lot range of normalcy—can anything ever be termed "constipation" or "diarrhea" in an infant? Yes, sometimes—and then a call to the doctor is in order. But the definitions are a little different from those you would apply to yourself.

Most babies grunt and turn red in the face when they are passing even a fairly soft stool; although it may seem to you that an extraordinary and uncalled-for amount of effort has been expended, this is a perfectly normal state of affairs and no cause for alarm. Some babies—chiefly, though not exclusively, bottle-fed babies—will depart from their usual soft-stool pattern every once in a while and produce a stool that is quite firm; if the baby doesn't cry out in pain when he's passing such a stool, or otherwise seem ill, he is not constipated, and nothing needs to be done.

Your clues to true constipation lie, essentially, in *combinations* of unusually firm or infrequent stools (unusual, that is, for *your* child) with *other* symptoms. You should be concerned, and should call your doctor, if your baby seems bloated and in distress, and you think it might be because he hasn't moved his bowels recently; or if he is in obvious pain when passing an atypically hard stool. You should also hasten to get medical care for a small baby whose abdomen is definitely distended, whose infrequent stools are very large and accompanied by much effort and distinct distress, and who at other times produces a good deal of odorous gas (with, possibly, small amounts of liquid fecal material); these could be symptoms of a serious—but correctable—congenital problem.

How about diarrhea? The definition is even trickier here, and it *is* important for you to recognize true diarrhea when it occurs; just because babies are the size they are, diarrhea can cause a dangerous amount of liquid loss in a relatively short time, and extreme dehydration can be a life-threatening condition. You will not find the dictionary of much help. "An abnormal frequency of intestinal discharge" (Merriam-Webster) hardly clarifies matters. If your baby usually has five bowel movements a day, and one day he has seven—is that diarrhea? What if he has nine? Or six, but they're very loose?

Dictionary definitions aside, diarrhea—like constipation—does not refer either to stool consistency or to frequency of movements alone. You will be safe, so far as your child's health—and your own peace of mind—are concerned, if you adopt, as your practical definition of diarrhea: stools that are looser and more watery than normal (for *your* baby), *and* more frequent than normal (for *your* baby), *in a baby who is otherwise not acting well.* "Otherwise not acting well" might include such things as vomiting, or a distinct loss of appetite, or an indication that the child is in pain, or simply a feeling on your part (such feelings can usually be trusted) that the baby is "not quite himself." True diarrhea is commonly a symptom of some infection or other disturbance in the gastrointestinal tract, and it demands prompt medical diagnosis and treatment.

Loose stools alone, on the other hand, frequently stem from two other sources.

One is teething. Some babies, though not all, tend to have consistently loose stools each time a new tooth begins working its way through the gum. The reason is probably that a generous amount of saliva is being secreted and a lot of it finds its way into the intestines, diluting the material there. As soon as the tooth has erupted, the baby's stools regain their normal consistency. If your baby produced loose stools the first time around, the odds are very good that he'll do the same with the eruption of his other nineteen baby teeth. (If it is *not* yet a predictable pattern, do call your doctor; infection should be ruled out before you conclude that your baby is about to produce a tooth.)

Secondly, lots of babies—and quite a few adults, for that matter—are susceptible to something doctors call a "parenteral diarrhea," a mysterious phrase meaning simply that the trouble is basically not in the intestines but somewhere else. Usually the somewhere else is the upper respiratory tract and the trouble is an ordinary cold. Unusual amounts of mucus are secreted by the nasal membranes; some of that mucus is swallowed and finds its way to the intestinal tract, producing looser stools and—because the mucus irritates the tract—more frequent stools. Rarely does the transient diarrhea itself represent any real problems. But it should be called to your doctor's attention, since treatment may be needed for the underlying infection, wherever it may be.

Finally—and it is one of the things that make pediatrics, and parenthood, so challenging (or, sometimes, exasperating)—some babies don't fall into any of those nice, neat categories. I have known many babies who produced loose stools from time to time for no discernible reason; they did not have any infections in their guts or noses or elsewhere, and they were not teething either. I have even known some who always had loose stools, all through infancy, but who gained weight well, continued to thrive, and grew to be strong, healthy children; that seemed to be *their* "normal" pattern, at least for that particular period of life.

Stage 1½: "When Are You Going to Train the Baby?"

None of my patients has ever gone to kindergarten in diapers. Extensive inquiry among my colleagues reveals that their experience has been similar.

That knowledge will, I hope, help to sustain you when you begin to be interrogated—and you will be—by friends and relatives. You will be asked why Johnny, age two, who appears to be "such a *big* boy," is still in diapers, with the clear implication that Johnny must be terribly backward. You will be urged to compare your child with others, often with subtly unflattering insinuations about *your* capability ("Oh, Michael's three? I had Charles out of diapers at two and a half!"). This sort of thing can lead to deep brooding, and you may even begin asking *yourself* questions, especially if it is not your first child ("Susie was out of diapers at two, and now Steven's almost three . . .").

I have often wondered why people who would not think of inquiring about another adult's elimination habits feel perfectly free to pry into such personal matters where a child is concerned—often, in the child's hearing. It seems to me there are far more interesting topics for discussion among grown-ups.

You should know, in any event, that there is absolutely no connection between your child's intelligence—or yours, for that matter—and the age at which he is able to handle his own elimination. Some youngsters do, indeed, achieve full control by the age of two; they are rare. Others will not be ready to do so until their fourth birthday is approaching. Both are perfectly normal, as are all the times in between. Children in all societies eventually learn to follow the prevailing toileting customs of those around them—even if their parents do and say absolutely nothing about it; I promise you that your child will not be the first recorded exception. And I can assure you too that you will not recall, as you are weeping at his wedding, whether he was toilet-trained at twenty-six months, thirty-two months, or forty-four months.

An understanding of just what's involved, physiologically

speaking, can also help you to develop a more relaxed attitude.

Babies learn to master their muscles gradually, and that control always proceeds—at whatever speed, and it is quite variable—in a head-to-toe direction. That is, a child will pick up his head before he can roll over, roll over before he can pull himself up to standing position, stand before he can walk, and so on. Speech does not occur until this neuromuscular process is fairly well advanced. And compared with these things, control of elimination is extraordinarily complex.

Consider, for a moment, what going to the bathroom involves for you, or for any adult. You must (1) feel the sensation of a full bowel or bladder; (2) interpret the significance of that sensation; (3) issue neural instructions to the sphincters, or circular muscles, that control the elimination route; (4) contract those sphincters; (5) walk—or, as the case may be, run—to the appropriate location; (6) perform necessary disrobing; (7) release the sphincters so that urination or defecation may take place. Astonishing, isn't it? You really *do* do all these things each time you go to the bathroom! And they are, of course, second nature now—automatic, as it were. But now, apply them to your child—and realize that there is still a further step that precedes them: somehow, he must make the connection between the sensation and the results —that is, a wet or soiled diaper.

Once that has happened, you may begin to hope that the first four steps will follow. All you *can* do is hope. None of these steps is remotely under your control. Remember, too, that when they have taken place another factor enters the picture: the child must be able to *communicate* this new concept. If a child cannot talk, he cannot tell you he has to go; if he does not tell you, you will have no way of knowing it is time to rush him into the bathroom.

There have been a few recorded cases of children who have not yet learned to talk devising ways of communicating the need to eliminate. I recall one eleven-month-old girl who gave forth an odd sort of grunt while I was examining her in my office. "She has to go to the bathroom," her mother informed me—and so she did. I watched, astonished, as her mother lifted her down from the examining table, followed as she carried the child into the bathroom and set her on the toilet—where she proceeded to urinate. At some point, the child's mother explained, the infant had devised this signal, and it worked beautifully, because it was perfectly clear to both of them.

Pediatricians remember such youngsters precisely because they are so rare. I would advise you not to count on your child's proving to be one of those exceptions to the rule.

Stage 2: Trials and Errors

You have already gathered, I trust, that there is no predicting when a child will be ready to begin the process of training himself—which is really what the process is. But the day will come. *Really.*

Typically, the dawning of awareness is signaled by an after-the-fact announcement—i.e., some sort of verbal message—that the child is wet or soiled: he has detected an uncomfortable situation, and he actually conveys that discovery to you. He may be under two when this happens, but it is more likely that he will be over two, or even past three. Children who are especially annoyed by wet or soiled diapers tend to reach this point at an earlier age than children who are not. This announcement is a very encouraging sign; being aware of a problem is always the first step toward solution.

The thing to do at this point is, of course, to change him. And to suggest quietly that there is actually a way to avoid the discomfort entirely, that he might "try to tell Mommy, next time, if you think you're going to go; that way, you can use the toilet." He will try. But do not confidently expect that this prescience will operate the very next time. It won't; the odds, at least, are against it. Probably the same episode will occur again. And again. Be patient. And repeat the same advice, in the same tone of voice.

Bear in mind that, by this time, he *wants* to be free of the discomfort. He also wants to behave like others, to acquire grown-up skills. If he has older siblings, he is probably aware of how and where they eliminate. Most youngsters, at this stage, have toddled into the bathroom behind their mothers or fathers and made curious inquiries; now it is beginning to occur to your child that he, too, may be capable of these feats. But both you and he must wait for those physiological developments I mentioned earlier. It will not help matters to intimidate him, to tell him that he must perform to please you, to insist that he instantly acquire the skills of his older brother.

There *will* come a time, just as you have almost abandoned hope, when he will actually announce the event ahead of time. The thing to do then is simply say, "Oh? Good. We'll go to the bathroom. That's the place to do it." The thing not to do is jump up and down, clap your hands in obvious glee, and announce the event to your nearest neighbor.

Why not any fanfare?

While a certain amount of praise is due (it is, after all, an accomplishment), it should be carefully phrased—along the lines of "I knew you could do it," rather than "How absolutely fantastic!" A child who is greeted with the latter sort of reception can easily retreat into a defensive I'm-not-trying-*that*-again attitude, since it will be obvious to anyone that the last smash performance could not possibly be topped, and probably not even equaled. This prospect may well frighten him, and that fright could lead to one of the most unpleasant problems in pediatrics: voluntary stool-holding (he can now control his sphincters, remember). This problem, believe me, is infinitely easier to prevent than cure.

While we are on the subject of psychology, this is as good a time as any to make what I think are a couple of other vital points.

I trust it is your hope, not to have your child out of diapers at an age that will please Aunt Martha, but to see that he eventually is able to handle his elimination in the way our society expects him to—cleanly, efficiently, without ado and without assistance, in a manner that will disturb neither him nor those around him. To do that, it is desirable for him to have a clear idea of the place of this process in his life.

As I have pointed out, we eat food—assuming we have no distorted idea of its function—consciously because we feel hungry, physiologically because it is needed to fuel the activities of our brains and bodies. We use what we need and discard the rest. Urine and stools are simply the by-products of the body's metabolism, to be disposed of in whatever manner society generally agrees is appropriate. It is well to be sure your child is not confused on this point; any implication that toileting (a term I prefer to "toilet training," since the latter suggests a formal program of instruction) has any significance beyond this *can* give him misleading ideas.

One way to do this is for you to hint that his elimination is a moral issue. Your anxious "Come on, honey, be good and see if you can go for Mommy" tells a youngster that you care, deeply; his elimination thereafter becomes a matter of mind over Mommy. Remember that you can lead a child to the toilet but you can't make him go; *he* is the one who controls—or is learning to control—those vital sphincters. The anal sphincter, as any adult knows, is controllable to a high degree, once one gets the hang of it. Defecation viewed as a moral duty can become a weapon in a clash of wills, and often does: the child will use it "against" you as a sort of reverse temper tantrum—withholding it if he wants to annoy you, performing to win your approval.

This is not good for a child physically.

Children who get the idea that what goes in at one end or comes out at the other has some bearing on whether or not they are loved also often grow up with strange notions about their relationships with other people, as many busy psychiatrists can testify.

Another method of creating a monster is making your child's normal bodily functions topics of major household concern. Children naturally and normally want their parents' attention as much as possible. Once a child has discerned that you place undue importance upon toileting, he will be shrewd enough to employ it as an effective attention-getting device. He will decide that he has had enough of your bridge game, or your phone conversation, or your perusal of the evening paper. He will toddle into the room and announce, "I have to go to the bathroom, Mommy (or Daddy)!" Mommy or Daddy will immediately leave whatever he or she is doing, scoop him up, rush him into the bathroom, undo all his clothing, and place him on the seat. After a few minutes he will smile beguilingly and say, "I guess maybe I don't have to go."

If he has not gotten any mistaken idea, and is simply requesting your assistance, fine. Help him. It is not necessary to behave as if the house were on fire; the worst that can happen, after all, is that he soils his diapers or pants—which is not likely to happen if he has developed enough control to get to wherever you are with his message. (After he is able to handle the whole procedure by himself, any such announcements need not—and should not—interrupt your activities at all, and the appropriate answer is, "Fine—go ahead, dear." In a strange or public place, of course, you should point out the bathroom or accompany him.)

Somewhere along the line you will contemplate the purchase of a potty seat. You will wonder whether that is better than a small seat that fits on top of the regular adult toilet. It really doesn't make any difference, from any health standpoint. Each has advantages and disadvantages. The important thing is that the child feels comfortable—which he will on a potty seat, because it is specially built for people his size; his feet will be resting on the floor, and the typical potty seat has armrests as well. Of course you will have to do the emptying, unless and until you think you can trust the child to do it.

A special seat on the adult toilet immediately introduces a child to the use of that device and accustoms him to the flushing mechanism, which is good. But you should provide a step stool that the child can climb up on and rest his feet on while he is sitting; if a youngster is simply set on such a high perch, with his feet dangling, he is not going to feel either comfortable or secure—and a boy, of course, must have a place to stand when he urinates.

Further, some such seats do not have arms. If a child is afraid of falling off the seat, he can hardly concentrate on the business at hand, and it is very likely that he will develop a deep aversion to using the seat. If you decide upon this method, it would be a kind gesture on your part—and, in the long run, helpful to you—to provide something that he can clutch, such as a nearby sink, a towel bar, or a projecting toilet-paper dispenser.

Bear in mind, whichever you choose, the complications of away-from-home toileting. A child who has been used to his own potty seat generally must be graduated to at-home use of the toilet before he will be willing to try one elsewhere. If a youngster has been using a special seat on the regular toilet, you can of course carry that seat with you wherever you go, but I really don't think that's necessary; most children will be amenable to using a strange toilet—*if* you stand by and hold them so they don't feel insecure.

There is only one other facet of the learning-to-go period that requires any concern on your part—which it does, because your youngster's health is involved.

We all harbor within us populations of tiny organisms of various types; one especially heavily populated area is the lower intestine. Among the residents of that region are an assortment of bacteria. They have every right to be there; they are in fact both necessary and helpful, assigned to such useful pursuits as the decomposition of waste products into forms that can be, and are, excreted. Should they find their way to some other part of the body, however, they are potential mischief-makers, and their presence signifies not the nicely balanced ecology of the gut but an infection.

Bacteria, being extremely low-level organisms, cannot be expected to know their proper place. It therefore becomes the responsibility of higher-level organisms, such as you and me, to see that they do not find their way to sites—such as the mouth or respiratory tract—where they might stir up trouble.

Specifically, this means that one's hands must be promptly washed, with soap and water, after dealing with the results of a bowel movement—whether one's own or someone else's. It is important that you impress the necessity of this upon your youngsters. It is also important, if your child is a girl, to see that she learns to do her wiping in the right direction —toward the back, *away* from her urinary tract and her vagina, which are other places in which fecal bacteria could trigger infection; the tissue should be discarded after each swipe and a fresh piece used for the next one (don't rub back and forth).

One not uncommon complaint I hear from parents of little boys—less often, of girls—is that they consistently urinate in the toilet without any help from anyone but ask to have a diaper put on when they feel they are going to have a bowel movement. Most little boys enjoy the process of urinating "like Daddy": it is totally visible, under their own control, and in fact rather fun; but when they have to sit down, and do not see the stool coming out but merely hear it plop into the bowl, they rebel. Perhaps it is a fear of losing part of themselves (as some psychologists have theorized); perhaps they are alarmed by the sound of solid matter hitting water; perhaps it is just *because* the process takes place "behind their backs," as it were. In any event, they prefer to cling to the familiarity of diapers to defecate.

Annoying and messy as this may be to parents, I think it is preferable to accede to the request for diapers rather than have the child withhold his stool entirely or deposit the stool in some out-of-the-way place in or around the house. With patience and encouragement on your part, he will eventually get over his aversion to the toilet. Staying with him while he has his bowel movement will help. You might also try putting several sheets of crumpled toilet paper in the bowl first, so that the stool will fall softly on top; let the child inspect it—without any gratuitous comments from you—and then let him flush it down himself.

There will come a time—no parent of a first child ever believes me, but it's true—when your child will be out of diapers, when both bladder and bowels will be under control (boys, as noted, often achieve bladder control first; with girls, it's frequently the opposite). It has been known to happen literally overnight, with the sudden announcement, "Now I am too grown up for diapers, and I don't need them any more." And he doesn't! Don't heave too ecstatic a sigh of relief. The marathon is not quite over. But you *are* in the homestretch.

Stage 3: Accidents Will Happen

Many parents wonder why the child who has full bladder control when he is awake often wets at night, even sometimes during a long nap. The reasons are fairly simple. You must realize that the production of urine proceeds around the clock. Which means that the bladder is constantly filling; a full bladder means that urination will, voluntarily or involuntarily, follow. Children are at a special disadvantage because their bladders, like the rest of them, are so small; boys —whether newborn or full-grown—are at a particular disadvantage, because they have a relatively smaller bladder capacity than girls do.

In short, when your bladder is full—assuming you can detect that condition, which takes some practice—you have got to move pretty fast. The smaller you are, the more frequently this race against time will take place. If you are a small boy, it is likely to happen even more often.

Daytime control of this process invariably takes place before nighttime control—and even so, accidents can occasionally occur. I don't think you ought to insult a youngster by putting him back into diapers, once they have been abandoned for daytime. There are several things you *can* do, however, that will make life easier for both of you.

You can, for instance, put waterproof pants on a recently graduated youngster if he is going to be outdoors for longer than he can reasonably be expected to control himself. I certainly would suggest you do so in winter, particularly. Without such protection, he could well flood several layers of clothing, not to mention his socks and boots, and be thoroughly chilled and very uncomfortable. It is also a dreary chore for you to take care of cleaning and laundering those snow pants, socks, boots, etc.

You can see that the youngster wears clothing, indoors or

out, that is easy for him to get out of fast. Overalls, for example, are not a very good bet at this stage. And don't rush a boy into fly-front underpants—unless he puts in a definite request for them. While I think a boy should be wearing fly-fronts when he enters first grade, boys under five generally find them very hard to manipulate. You would be surprised how many five-year-olds who have been supplied with fly-front pants regularly put them on backward and are totally unaware that they have done so. It's much more economical to leave him in training pants until they wear out.

You can also anticipate the possibility of accidents under certain conditions. Your youngster cannot be blamed if, in the middle of a shopping trip, he suddenly tells you, "I have to go, Mommy," and you realize to your horror that there is not a rest room anywhere in sight, and he has an accident. You can only sympathize, and that is all you should do; believe me, he feels as miserable about it as you would if it had happened to you (and such mishaps are not totally unheard of among grownups). Before the next shopping trip, or any extended trip anywhere, you might take the precautionary step of telling him, "We are going to be out for a long time, so you will go to the bathroom—*now*."

If a child can cope well enough during the day but has never managed to stay dry all night, it is probably for one of two reasons, or more likely both: (1) his bladder capacity just isn't large enough yet for him to wait that long; and (2) he sleeps so soundly that the sensation of a full bladder fails to awaken him. One thing you can do, and it occurs to most parents sooner or later, is to see that he urinates just before he goes to bed—and that he doesn't get any fluids after that. Another is to hustle him into the bathroom the moment he wakes up; a good deal of apparent nighttime wetting actually occurs during the few minutes of that fuzzy state between fast asleep and fully alert. Often, neither of these ploys works, and the child keeps wetting during the night. What to do then?

Generally, it depends on the child's age. Daytime control is typically achieved by the time a youngster is three or three and a half, perhaps a bit later. Nighttime control may coincide or, more commonly, follow a few months later—that is, by four or four and a half. If bed wetting is still continuing after that, as an every-night or almost-every-night affair (not just an occasional accident), do not panic; it's true of about one in eight four-to-five-year-olds. But it *is* a good idea to talk the question over with your doctor. Doctors have varying opinions on how to cope with this question; since this is my book, what follows are my opinions.

I do not think awakening the child in the middle of the night and leading him—half asleep—to the bathroom to perform is particularly effective. Aside from the fact that he will probably be oblivious to what is going on, most of them seem to wet again anyway, so the bed is not going to be dry unless he is dragged to the bathroom two or three times. If you are an incurable insomniac, and this would give you something to do during those long, sleepless hours, you might like to try it. Most parents I know would prefer to get a good night's rest.

Some physicians favor the use of mechanical devices—one is called an Enurotone—which, placed beneath the child, ring a loud bell at the first drop of urine. I do not. It is totally beyond the youngster's control, extremely shocking and, in my view, a rather dastardly thing to do to a human being.

Another quite different kind of mechanical awakener, however, enlists the child's cooperation, understanding, and agreement and is a rather good device to try if the child is old enough. I allude to the ordinary alarm clock. There are a great many attractive, cheery-looking ones available, and most youngsters think that having a personal clock of their own is a very grown-up privilege. I think it's a good idea to let the child go with you and help pick it out. Make it one with a loud ring.

Set the clock for about halfway through the night, or before whatever hour you believe the wetting occurs, whichever is earlier. Place it across the room from the child's bed, so that he will have to get up, and show him how to shut it off. It is understood that, having done so, he will go to the bathroom and urinate, and then go back to bed.

If you have discovered that he wets more than once during the night, then set the alarm for an earlier hour, before you plan to go to bed (if the child retires at 8:00, and you'll be up until 12:00, then set the clock for, say, 11:45). After the child goes to the bathroom and returns to bed, reset the alarm for four or five o'clock or whatever hour you think will catch him before the second wetting.

None of this is going to be very helpful if the child sleeps so soundly that the alarm leaves him snoozing peacefully while jolting everyone else in the house awake. In that case, there is another recourse, which works for some 50 to 75 percent of young bed wetters.

This is a medication that goes by the chemical name of imipramine. It was actually developed for quite another purpose, but—like a number of other substances—it works differently in children. In adults, it acts as an antidepressant. In children, its effect—for reasons we frankly don't fully understand—is to increase bladder capacity, thus letting the youngster sleep through the night without wetting. Unfortunately, it is not available in liquid form; the child must be able to get a tablet down. If the child himself is annoyed about his bed wetting and is eager to try and stop it, it's worth your while to teach him the art of pill swallowing. (This is not, by the way, an over-the-counter drug; it must be prescribed by your doctor.)

Very often, incidentally, a youngster who still has a wetting problem in his own bed will not have accidents in
strange beds, such as those in hotel rooms or in the homes of
friends or relatives. That's because he is less comfortable,
and sleeps less soundly, in unfamiliar surroundings. In this
sort of situation, if a light is left on so that he can find his way
to a bathroom, he will usually get up and go there if the
urge to urinate comes on during the night. If the place is one
the child knows very well, however, he may feel just as comfortable, and sleep just as deeply, as he does at home—and
wet the bed just as much, too.

The awesome medical term "enuresis" is one you may have
seen applied to the problems we have been discussing. It
should not be. Enuresis is indeed a condition demanding professional medical attention, and it is properly applied only
to the child who suddenly begins to lose control, especially
at night, *after* he had been consistently dry for some time,
or to the child who *continues* to be a steady bed wetter after
the age of five. There are many disorders that could be at the
root of the trouble; possibilities include diabetes, as well as
infection in the urinary tract. It is up to your pediatrician or
family doctor to determine the precise nature of the problem
and to prescribe appropriate treatment.

If your youngster has achieved full bladder and bowel control on his own initiative, you need not be afraid that he will
revert to baby toileting behavior under psychological stress,
despite dire warnings you may have read to the contrary.
Since he does not have the idea that he is using the toilet to
please you, or for some other mixed-up reason, a child does
not regress when you bring home a new baby, when he goes
to the hospital, or when some other event occurs to disrupt
familiar household routine.

4

Sometimes It's a Long, Long Way to the Land of Nod

There is perhaps no area—with the possible exception of vitamin pills—in which myth has been so persistent as that of sleep needs. So far as adults are concerned, personal experience has pretty much succeeded in dispelling the old-time reliance on the sacred number eight; as we all discover, some of us function perfectly well with only four hours of sleep each night, while others need a good deal more—nine hours or even ten.

Yet concerning infants and children the myth lingers on. Pronouncement after pronouncement, by presumed child-care authorities, continues to spell out sleep needs—to the hour, and sometimes in fractions thereof—for children of various ages. I have on my desk, as I write, a recent (1971) textbook that solemnly declares sleep requirements to be fourteen to fifteen hours for two-year-olds, thirteen to fourteen hours for three-year-olds, and eleven to twelve hours for four-year-olds. To be strictly enforced, presumably, from birthday to birthday.

Actually, children vary in their sleep needs—just as adults do. A number of studies have substantiated this fact.

Infants, of course, sleep just as much as they need to, no more and no less. In one definitive study, 75 newborn infants were observed continuously for seventy-two hours, starting at the moment they were born. The average amount of sleep per twenty-four-hour period: sixteen and a half hours—but the figure for some of the babies was as low as ten and a half, and the top time registered was an astounding twenty-three hours out of twenty-four! I assure you that none of these babies was staying up to watch television or otherwise dissuaded or distracted from getting the sleep he needed and wanted—nor were any of the infants under sedation.

Other studies have surveyed other age groups in the preschool range. One, for example, examined two-and-a-half-year-olds; they were found to sleep anywhere from less than eight to more than fourteen hours at night (average, eleven hours), with the total sleep time for a twenty-four-hour period, including daytime naps, averaging thirteen hours—but ranging from eight to seventeen. Another, conducted at the University of Minnesota, mapped the sleep patterns of more than 1,000 preschool youngsters and came up with quite similar findings; this study concluded, further, that the eleven-hours-per-night average (*average*, remember, by no means representing all normal children) remained consistent right through the preschool years. Yes, youngsters do need less sleep, in general, as they grow from infancy to kindergarten age, and total sleeping time per twenty-four hours will decrease if children are left to their own devices. The difference lies primarily in *daytime* sleep needs.

Babies under one year generally need some sleep morning and afternoon, as well as at night; by the time they're about two—more or less—most children don't really need the morning nap (if they still want it, fine—but don't insist). Most youngsters do continue to need some nap time during the afternoon; that need averages out at about an hour and a half at the age of one year, tapering down to half an hour at four (five-year-olds will generally refuse to do any daytime napping at all).

But again, I emphasize that these are strictly average figures—the results of studying the needs and habits of a great many youngsters. Many other patterns are fully within the range of normality. Thus, some two-year-olds may abandon the nap habit—either occasionally or completely. And at the other end of the scale, a four-year-old may enjoy two hours' sleep during the afternoon.

I might add, in case you are curious, that, try as they might to come up with correlations, researchers have found no significant differences in sleep needs between boys and girls. Nor are there any connections between sleep time and intelligence or any other factors.

"It Can't Be Bedtime, Because I'm Not in Bed Yet!"

I hope I have convinced you that you need not, and should not, insist that your child perform like a clock and tick off a specific number of sleeping hours per day. It *is* necessary, however, for you to get the child into a situation where he can get the sleep he needs, however much that may be. I.e., to bed. This is no problem whatever with a precrawler, who spends most of his time in his bed anyway, and will simply close his eyes and go to sleep when he is sleepy. The bedtime problem, and it can be a problem, arises with the child who is old enough to move around, talk—or at least listen to others talk—and be interested in the world around him. He has his own individual sleep needs; the difficulty is, essentially, in persuading him to recognize them.

A preschooler will often act sleepy when he is tired—if you can catch him off guard. A determined youngster can put up an amazingly stubborn fight against yawns and drooping eyelids if he is interested in what is going on and has made up his mind that he is not going to be sent to bed and miss something. It isn't a good idea to let things get to this stage, though; an overtired child actually finds it more difficult to get to sleep once he's in bed. (While a preschooler of any age usually takes about twenty minutes to fall asleep at nap time, and up to an hour at night, extreme fatigue can heighten his tension and lengthen that presleep period—thus, assuming the customary time of arising, shortening the period of actual sleep.) Children can and do make up for lost sleep, by the way—but not in one night; it usually requires a period of several days.

Getting down to specifics: how do you go about hustling Johnny off to bed—because you know very well from past experience that this is the right time for *him*, because of *his* sleep needs—when Johnny isn't having any of it? And why doth he protest so much?

One reason for his stubborn foot-dragging may be his limited understanding of the concept of time—past and future time, that is. It's rather difficult for an adult to grasp, but the fact is that small children simply do not conceive of time in nice, neat units like hours, days, and the like. Yesterday may just as well be last week—and next week, a hundred years from now. The famed Swiss child psychologist Jean Piaget has suggested that "bedtime" may, to a child, be a situation that simply does not occur until or unless one has actually reached it—i.e., that it can be deferred indefinitely so long as one stays away from one's bed. It is an interesting theory to contemplate, and one that might go a long way toward explaining why, in answer to your "It's bedtime, Johnny!" Johnny will defiantly reply, "No, not yet!" and go on playing with his blocks. Think about it.

Johnny does, of course, have to learn sometime. Besides, he does need his sleep. M. Piaget aside, Johnny will have to go to bed at a reasonable time, whether he is inclined to do so or not. It is up to you to select the time, based upon the time you know he will be getting up the next morning.

How you go about effecting the arrival of bedtime depends in part on the circumstances. I do not think it is quite fair, whatever Johnny may be doing, to suddenly swoop down upon him crying, "Okay, that's it! Bedtime! Now!" and haul him off; he will probably react with kicking and screaming, and I don't blame him. I would too.

It is nice to give him some warning. Something along the lines of, "Bedtime in ten minutes, Johnny. Start putting your toys away *now*." He may not know what "ten minutes" means—although if there is a clock handy, and he is verbal enough, you might suggest he note the position of the big hand—but he will get the idea that something is imminent. Let the child participate in the pre-bedtime procedures—putting things away, picking out a bedtime story, whatever is appropriate—but don't let him drag it out; you can be firm without being rigid.

If, incidentally, Johnny is really in the middle of something, and you know that if you let him stay up to finish it he *will* be overtired, tense, and cranky by the time he gets to bed, do not insist that he abandon it forever. Rather, let him know that you appreciate his activities—that he can finish coloring the picture the very first thing next morning, or that the tower he is building with his blocks will remain safely in a corner of the room and can be continued the next day. Reassure him about such things, if he seems doubtful; remember that "tomorrow" is a vague concept to a child and that "the minute you get up" may be more meaningful.

A word might be said, here, about another conceivable reason for a child's struggling to put off the bedtime scene. Something, that is, beyond the staving off of the future or the desire to continue a particular activity.

While his bed may—in a negative sense—represent a retirement from active participation in household activities, it should also, ideally, represent something positive: a place of rest, comfort, and security. A small child should be accom-

panied to bed—and tucked in, told a story, and/or whatever
you feel inclined to do—by his parent; bedtime should be
surrounded by a certain amount of affectionate parent-child
contact. A child's bed should not, on the other hand, become
a symbol of banishment or punishment; it is not a good idea
to use "I'll send you to bed" as a threat. If you have done so,
your child is likely to view ordinary directives to go to bed as
an indication that he has somehow transgressed. You—and
your child—do not need that kind of confusion.

Returning to the get-Johnny-to-bed problem. Sometimes
Johnny may be involved not in a self-contained play activity
but in group goings-on—such as a situation in which the
family is involved collectively. He will naturally be reluctant
to be arbitrarily removed from the group. Sometimes the wis-
est solution is to let him maintain some slender thread of
contact. You might, for example, permit him to doze off in
a corner of the family room, then tote him off to bed after
he's fallen asleep; I don't suggest this as a steady thing, rather
for some special occasions. Or you might take him to his own
bed but leave him some connection with activity he's loath
to leave—as by leaving the door of his room open—rather
than banish him completely from the scene.

By and large, I would advise you to accept—and enforce
firmly though not compulsively—the idea of a predetermined
bedtime hour, determined *by you*. But realize at the same
time that a child who is old enough to be involved in interesting activities—his or others'—deserves some consideration
too. And that sleep needs do gradually decrease. This generally does not affect nighttime needs in the preschool child
(as previously noted), but there are always exceptions. If
your youngster is beginning to wake up at 5:00 A.M. when he
previously slept until seven—a more convenient hour for you
—then chances are he can start retiring a little later.

Do not worry about lights or a reasonable level of noise
after you have laid your child to rest for the night. While sud-

den, strange noise—e.g., a violent argument or an explosion—
is likely to jar anyone awake, including a child, normal noise
will not. Neither the TV, nor the hubbub of a party in the
living room, nor the hall light left on, will keep an infant or
small child from falling asleep.

Fright in the Night

There are two phenomena that first-time parents should
know about—in case you don't recall experiencing them yourself. Maybe you didn't, and maybe your child won't, but a lot
of children do, and a cool, prepared head will be helpful.

One is nightmares, to which even adults are, of course, not
immune. Children are more susceptible to scary dreams because they're more impressionable and less experienced, and
they can easily be disturbed by stimuli an adult is capable of
ignoring.

The child who has had a nightmare will know why he has
awakened in a state of fright and will be able to recount his
dream experience. Encourage him to do so; don't just dismiss
his initial statement with, "Well, Michael, you know there
aren't any grizzly bears around here, so go back to sleep."
That simple dismissal has nowhere near the emotional impact of what he has just experienced. Of course he knows
your neighborhood isn't frequented by grizzlies. But that aca-
demic knowledge just isn't enough. Let him get the entire
dream off his chest; stay in his room, sit by his bed, and *listen*
while he relates it.

The object is to get the youngster back to safe reality—to
put the dream experience in perspective. Snickering at his
fear is not helpful; encourage *him* to see the absurdity of each
segment of the nightmare experience, so you can laugh at the
unreality of it together. He needs, initially, sympathy rather
than logic. It is good, too, to use *all* his senses in restoring his
sense of security. Have a light on while you talk; leave it on,

later, if he is more comfortable that way. Respond to his tale with firm reassurance as well as understanding and human sympathy. If, for example, he has—in his dream—found himself lost and abandoned, you might quickly comment, "Ooh, that *must* have been scary. Of course that couldn't really happen." *Physical* contact with reality is also important: it will help if you hold him in your arms while you talk.

A second, and completely different, kind of occurrence is a bit less likely to happen than a nightmare but is still not uncommon. If your child has waked up screaming and cannot tell you why—i.e., he is simply frightened and has no recollection of a bad dream—chances are he is a victim of what we call, for lack of a better term, *night terrors*. It may be that there *has* been a terrifying dream, and the youngster simply cannot recall it. But we suspect that this is a different phenomenon. And obviously, you cannot cope with it in exactly the same way, since you are dealing with pure fright. You may also be dealing with—again, not uncommonly—an alarming disorientation: the child may behave very strangely, and may not even appear to recognize you at first, when you run into his room in response to his screams.

Aside from the dream-recounting in the case of a nightmare, night terrors require much the same: reassurance and return to reality. Since your youngster may be acting somewhat irrational, your own first response may well be panic. I hope, for that reason, you are reading this before such an episode has occurred. Try to remain calm, and be patient. Ascertain that there is nothing physically wrong: ask if anything hurts (usually, nothing does). Then simply stay with the child and let him go back to sleep in your comforting presence. You may find, to your surprise, that he does not even remember the incident the next morning.

Night terrors—as opposed to nightmares—generally, I have found, do signal some emotional disturbance. But it is usually not of a deep-seated nature. It is a good idea to query the child the next day—subtly—to see if there is something special on his mind, something that he has been brooding over, something about which he feels insecure. As I have remarked before and will point out again, a small child's perceptions are not your perceptions. Because of his limited experience and knowledge, your child can very easily misinterpret situations—and react emotionally on the basis of those misinterpretations. I don't suggest that you draw up a couch, stretch the child out, take up a note pad, and intone, "Now, tell me what is bothering you." Simply make a point of conversing with the child and try to touch on a variety of subjects during the day; you may find that he will reveal an unsuspected source of fear or insecurity.

If you find that your child has night terrors often, or over an extended period of time, and you are at a loss to explain them, it's a good idea, then, to talk the question over with your pediatrician or family doctor. He or she may be able to pinpoint a problem that you cannot. And sometimes, though rarely, there is a more serious emotional problem, for which your doctor may feel professional help is needed.

All of the foregoing presupposes that you and the child can communicate verbally. If a child who cannot yet talk awakens in apparent fright, you will not and cannot be certain that he has had a nightmare. We believe that even infants as young as six months *may* experience nightmares, but there is of course no way to prove it. Parents' descriptions of such incidents, however, have been quite consistent: the baby awakens suddenly, with a cry that obviously expresses fright and not pain (parents always seem to sense the difference); the parent instinctively acts to provide comfort and reassurance, picking the infant up, rocking him, murmuring in a soothing tone of voice; the child soon relaxes and is able to fall asleep again.

You Can't Negotiate with a Nomad

Some children are nighttime wanderers. This does not mean that the child is either mentally disturbed or deliberately planning to annoy you; only that he awakens and is capable of moving about. Obviously, at this stage, the child is sleeping in something other than a crib—or he should be (I shall have some comment on the places-to-sleep question shortly). In a child who has been sleeping in a regular bed only a short time, that wandering often takes the form of arriving at his parents' bed—often at distinctly annoying or uncomfortable times—and pleading in a slightly trembly tone, "Mommy (and/or Daddy), can I sleep with you?"

I do not think this a good thing for Mommy and Daddy. Who, in the first place, need their sleep. It can also, obviously, interfere with the parents' sex life, which is not particularly good for the youngster either: to a three-year-old, the sex act might well appear aggressive and violent (and can give rise to nightmares). Thirdly, a youngster of this age often wets during the night, even if he is presumably fully trained; there is no need for you to invite such accidents in your own bed. If your youngster has started to do this, I strongly suggest you try rushing into his room at the first sign of a whimper—assuming, of course, that you can catch the whimper before he has left his own premises and shown up at your bedside. What you do, if you are successful, is sit with him *there* until he falls asleep—again, as with night terrors, first ascertaining if some physical problem, such as a pain or a need to go to the bathroom, has awakened him.

What if you cannot catch him before he has embarked on his ramblings? In my view, strict measures should be taken; you deserve your privacy. Further—quite another aspect of this problem—wandering children can be a danger to themselves. Some have wandered, for example, not to their parents' rooms but to the kitchen, where they have done such things as tinker with the stove or oven or other appliances. This sort of thing can result not only in serious injury to the child but in setting the whole place on fire. Obviously, these midnight rambles must be discouraged.

How to do so depends on both the child and his predilections. If his wanderings typically take him not to your bedroom but to the kitchen, say, or the garage, those obviously dangerous areas should be locked off. If your young nomad has a tendency to stroll into *your* room, you have another problem. You can lock the door of the child's room from the outside (leaving a potty chair inside, if he makes nighttime bathroom trips too). That idea may shake you, however. Although the youngster may not feel that he is a prisoner, *you* may feel that you are making him one. An alternative is to lock—or otherwise bar—your own door. If the child is capable of walking that far, he is also capable of rapping on the door in case he is really in trouble and needs your help.

If you are reading this before the problem has arisen, and the situation as I have described it looks hopeless (barring extreme measures), it may help you to know that it can often be headed off. I have known a number of families who have simply made it a "house rule" that bedroom doors be kept closed at all times and that anyone—child or adult—desiring access be required to knock before entering, be it midafternoon or 3:00 A.M. The rule is maintained, literally, at all times. No doors are actually locked. Thus, any member of the family—again, child or adult—is required to think, "Do I really want to disturb this person?" before entering anyone else's room, be it that of parent or sibling.

If your circumstances are such that not all members of the family enjoy exclusive right to their own rooms, the rule can still be applied: the privacy is then enjoyed jointly by whoever shares a particular room. Which still keeps out midnight ramblers from *your* room, no matter how your offspring may be doubled up.

The WHEREwithal

A great many parents, I find, seem concerned from the start about where their baby will sleep. The answer to that initial question is that he can sleep anywhere there is room.

A baby does not need a bassinet, a fancy crib, or some other sleeping place designed (presumably) for his needs. If you want him to have one, fine. But he doesn't need it, either physically or psychologically. What he needs is simply something that is big enough for him and that will shield him from danger. For a newborn baby, a dresser drawer or a large, old-fashioned wicker laundry basket functions beautifully. To be perfectly safe, it should be at least eight inches deep —*and* should be placed where an older sibling does not have ready access to it.

Sooner or later, if not immediately, you will probably have your baby sleep in a crib. If you are buying a new crib, I have no special advice. But if you plan to use an old, hand-me-down crib, there are two precautions you must take, for safety's sake. First, measure the distance between the bars. They should be *no more than three and one half inches apart*; infants have been strangled by thrusting their heads through larger openings (this admonition applies to your baby's playpen as well). The second concern is the paint; if it—the coat of paint, or the crib itself—dates from the 1960s or later, you can assume it's safe. If it is older, however, the paint may contain dangerous levels of lead, and it is a good idea to sand down the crib and repaint it.*

* When you purchase the paint, check the label. It should at least bear the legend "Conforms to American standard Z66.1-9 for use on surfaces that might be chewed by children"—meaning that the lead content is under one percent. This federal standard was set up in the late 1950s. Newer standards are even more stringent: paint intended for indoor use shipped by manufacturers after December 1972 may contain no more than 0.5 percent lead; for paint shipped after December 1973, the permissible maximum is 0.06 percent.

Your baby's crib, needless to say, should have sides that are high enough to keep the child, once he can pull himself erect, from falling out. Extensions are available for the long side—a good idea for tall tots who are inclined to reach beyond their capabilities. And don't get into the habit of keeping a huge stuffed panda, or any other toy that could be used as a booster for a child to stand on, in the crib.

The point of a crib, of course, is to keep your youngster safely confined, so that he will not clamber out and hurt himself. Once you know that your child *can* climb over the side, even with an extension, it makes little sense to insist that he sleep there. He may as well sleep in a regular bed; even if he does fall out (and it happens—usually with no calamitous results), it is a shorter distance to the floor from bed level than from crib level. If you're worried, you might like to place a thick rug—or a pile of pillows—beside the bed.

There is no sense, in my view, in spending your hard-earned money on something called a "junior bed." Let your child go from his crib to a regular bed—or whatever you expect him to use throughout his childhood years, be it full-scale mattress and box springs, bunk bed, roll-away cot, whatever.

If, on the other hand, your child's crib is a large one, and the child enjoys sleeping in it, I see no reason to push him into using a bed, so long as he doesn't want it and has not actually outgrown the crib. You may have another child on the way, and you may need the crib; in that case, it is wise to effect the first child's transfer well in advance, so that he does not get the impression that he is being physically displaced by the newcomer. But remember that the newborn sibling does not really need anything the size of a crib, and can be tucked in a basket, bassinet, dresser drawer, or some other suitable place for a while.

5

You Can't Keep a Child Clean, and Why Try

Babies are not subject to body odor. Hopefully, it will help you to reflect upon that fact. While *you* may find it desirable —and even necessary in order to avoid alienating your friends and colleagues, not to mention your spouse—to bathe or shower daily, infants and young children are not afflicted with that burden. It is only upon the advent of adolescence that the apocrine sweat glands—located, prominently, in the armpit and the crotch—become active; this activity, combined with the growth of hair in these areas (which entraps perspiration) and bacterial action, produces the aroma we have all come to know and loathe.

As a matter of fact, it will not harm your baby in the least if he or she is not bathed at all for the first six months of life. Not only do infants not have the dread "offending" problem; there is little likelihood—or, indeed, opportunity—of acquiring any significant amount of surface dirt during that period, at least on most of their bodies. I imagine, however, that despite these assurances you will feel obliged to cleanse your baby at intervals. I simply urge you to go to as little trouble as possible, so far as cleaning and grooming are concerned.

Your newborn baby's skin may be extremely dry and even cracked—a condition I often refer to as "dishpan body." This is because the child has been, essentially, waterlogged for nine months. Most parents realize—and they are right—that it will not help to add soap and water.

What they tend to do is smear on all sorts of lubricants. This is not necessary. It is not even desirable. Lubricants block the child's sweat glands, which may not be ready to function optimally anyway. You will do the infant a favor if you refrain from slathering oils and creams on his skin, and let his physical machinery become used to the new environment. The dryness and wrinkling will disappear in time.

Start at the Top—and Bottom

Although baths, per se, are not really needed, a certain amount of washing *is*. And some minimal grooming, as well. For purely physical reasons.

Medically, your baby should not be immersed in water until the tied-off umbilical cord has dropped off—which will occur after about a week or two. When that happens, you will find the child's navel is rather messy-looking—moist, and possibly blood-tinged. This is normal; do not be alarmed. Simply daub the area, once a day, with regular rubbing alcohol. That helps to dry it up. The baby will generally squeal—not because the alcohol burns or otherwise causes discomfort, but simply because it is unexpectedly cold.

Three other areas—four, if your baby is a girl—do need special attention, whether or not the baby is ready for total immersion.

One is the scalp. It is children whose heads are not properly cleaned who are victims of the distasteful ailment called cradle cap: a condition in which greasy, yellowish crusts form on the scalp. Soap (any mild soap is fine) and water on a soft washcloth, applied once a week (more frequent washing is not necessary), will prevent cradle cap; you may want to use a piece of soft flannel rather than a regular washcloth, and that's fine. Don't be afraid you'll hurt the misnamed "soft spot." It's true that the skull bones haven't fused completely. But nature has provided a remarkably tough, leathery membrane to protect the area in the meantime; it would take a great deal of effort with a sharp instrument to penetrate it, so don't worry that you might do so by accident.

The second area that does need periodic washing is the baby's bottom. Bowel movements are indeed occasions for cleansing; feces contain bacteria that are potential troublemakers if they are permitted to remain on the skin. Again, the best thing to use is mild soap and water; apply a lubricant, such as petroleum jelly, lotion, or powder, if you like, to soothe the area afterward.

In a newborn girl, there is usually a thick, whitish material between the inner and outer labia (the vulva). Do *not* scrub it off; it will gradually wear away and disappear. If the area becomes contaminated with stool, simply clean it gently with a piece of wet cotton, wiping once toward the anus. Discard the cotton after one swipe. Repeat until the area is clean.

There is one other grooming necessity right at the start: your baby's fingernails must be cut—partly because they provide a place for dirt to accumulate, but mostly because babies are given to scratching themselves and poking curiously at their eyes, ears, and genitals. They can thus do themselves all kinds of damage, and trigger nasty infections to boot. It is best to keep the fingernails trimmed quite short all through childhood, for this reason.

Do the trimming with a small scissors, clipper, or whatever you feel comfortable with. Some parents are leery about handling scissors near a baby; if you prefer an emery board, fine. The time to do the trimming is following a feeding, when the child has dropped contentedly off to sleep (if he starts to fidget before you've finished all ten nails, just stop; next nap, continue where you left off). Cut or file the nails straight across, and be careful not to leave sharp corners.

Don't worry about toenails. They grow far more slowly than fingernails and almost never need cutting until a child is around two years old—if then.

When the Cord Goes ("*Look, Ma, I'm Immersible!*")

We come, now, to the immersible baby—the one whose umbilical cord has dropped off. How often need/should you bathe him? As I've pointed out, you needn't bathe him at all. But you will probably want to. And perhaps it should be noted that bathing may, at this age, serve quite another purpose.

Most babies love baths: they enjoy the water, and the splashing, and the adventure of the experience. (If your baby seems to hate the procedure, or you feel insecure about it yourself, do put it off; as I've noted, it will do no harm.) You may want to start giving your child baths as soon as the umbilical cord has dropped off, even if he doesn't really need one. At this point, you may begin to wonder about the mechanics.

I feel that bathinets are a real nuisance, unless you happen to have an extra bathtub in which the thing can be set up— where you can fill it from the shower above and let it drain into the tub below. If you have to fill it by carrying pails of water, and drain it via similarly tedious toting of water, or set it up in the tub each time you decide to use it, I don't think it's worth the effort. The height is usually bad as well, necessitating your bending uncomfortably at the same time as you are trying to hold the baby securely.

I suggest you choose one of two other alternatives. One is

the kitchen sink. This means you will not need to go to any extra expense. You will, however, need to be alert; you must be sure the child neither hits a faucet—thus triggering a spout of possibly scalding water—nor strikes his head (or any other part of his body) on any of the plumbing. A second choice is a plastic tub or dishpan—generally available at low cost— which you can fill at the kitchen sink, then place on a counter or table of convenient height; choose, of course, a size that will fit the child.

A wet baby is a slippery baby. A wet, *soapy* baby is even more slippery. Remember that a baby who cannot yet sit up by himself must be propped up by you; never permit his face to slip under water. The main secret of bathing a baby safely is to wash one section at a time, leaving yourself something to grip that's relatively unslippery. Soap and rinse one arm, while firmly clutching the other; then do the other arm, then the front, then the back, and so on. (For a baby's face, by the way, soap is not needed; plain water will do.) You should continue to use a washcloth (or, again, soft flannel if you like) on the scalp; I suggest you just use your own hand for the rest. The actual washing operation takes about two minutes. But the splashing and kicking will take longer, and I urge you to let the baby enjoy himself; it's fun, it's a learning experience, and it's good exercise besides.

This is as good a place as any to go into the shampoo question, since some babies manage to sprout an astounding amount of hair in an amazingly short time (though the majority do not).

When there is a good deal of hair, a liquid preparation—i.e., a shampoo—is just easier to use than a bar of soap; easier and faster to rinse out, too. Once a week is quite often enough to shampoo a baby's hair, so long as he hasn't plopped several handfuls of puréed carrots, or something like that, on his head; if he hates shampoos violently you can even let it go a little longer.

Most babies do not care to have their heads washed, though the degree of dislike may vary. And they do not like baby shampoo in their eyes any more than any other kind (though baby shampoo—or some other mild type—is preferable because it is gentler to the hair and scalp). Do everything you can to keep the soap out of the child's eyes and—of course—the child's nose out of the water. You can try a shampoo shield—a plastic, elasticized affair that stands out from the head like a broad hatbrim and, hopefully, prevents any shampoo from dribbling down onto the child's face; you might have a little trouble, though, finding one that will fit securely and also stay in place. When the youngster is old enough, you can of course enlist his cooperation; he can hold a damp, folded washcloth tightly over his closed eyes during the shampooing.

Two other areas need special mention.

If your child's healed navel is the tucked-in kind, it requires some minimal attention. About once a week, either in the bath or while changing the baby, spread the puckers apart and cleanse the navel with either soap and water, or alcohol on a piece of cotton (you will *not* hurt the baby). If you don't do this, skin secretions and urine from the diapers will accumulate, and after a while there will be an odor; this material may also produce irritation, or even infection, in the surrounding area.

Second, the penis of an *un*circumcised boy needs care. At birth, the foreskin is very adherent and cannot be retracted. After a couple of months the secretions between the glans and the foreskin become less tenacious, and it is possible to begin to gently retract the foreskin. This should be done at least once a day. Pull it back as far as you can without hurting the baby. If it cannot be retracted fully after two or three

months—that is, by the time he is five or six months old—
mention it to your doctor, who will be able to perform the
retraction. Once the foreskin can be fully retracted, continue
to retract it at least once daily, and keep it up until the
child begins to do it himself—which he *will* do, when he is
masturbating regularly (100 percent of boys do masturbate,
as do ninety-nine out of a hundred girls).

If that retraction is not done, the secretions—called
smegma—will re-accumulate and cause the foreskin to adhere.
Occasionally, infection occurs under the adherent foreskin,
resulting in a great deal of distress—sometimes including inability to urinate, and necessitating emergency surgical procedures. The vast majority of boys never run into this
problem, but it is advisable to keep this area very clean, to
avoid even the possibility of trouble.

When your infant is about six months old, more or less
(perhaps not until he's nearly a year old), he'll begin to be
mobile. The way babies get around at first is on their hands
and knees. Once a baby is crawling, it is impossible to keep
him clean all the time. Show me a child who has reached
this stage and is constantly immaculate, and I will show you
a child who is not permitted any freedom at all. If you want
him to appear even fairly clean, you will have to wash his
hands, his face, his feet (if they are not covered), and his
knees (if he's just wearing diapers) several times a day.

I urge you, as I have done earlier and will undoubtedly do
again, not to waste your time performing unnecessary tasks.
If you want to remove the dirt before you deposit him in his
nice clean crib, fine. If your mother-in-law is about to arrive
on a cross-country flight for her first glimpse of the new
grandchild—sure, clean him up a bit, if you think Grandma
will be upset by his soiled condition. Otherwise, don't bother,
beyond a daily (or almost daily) bath.

Baby, Meet Bathtub

At some point your baby will become too big for the kitchen sink or the plastic dishpan. Now he's ready to be introduced to the real bathtub. This will be a big change for him. While he has grown large in relation to the plastic dishpan or kitchen sink, he is quite small vis-à-vis the bathtub. He can also slip around—dangerously.

It is important to secure him somehow. You can get a small immersible chair for just this purpose; it has suction cups on the bottom and can be placed wherever you like. There are also handy little stick-on skidproofing sets—strips, flower-shaped cut-outs, etc.—with nonslip surfaces; they are very good for children and adults alike, and will serve to keep a child anchored without investing in extra equipment. Position your youngster, whether on chair or those special stick-ons, as far away from the faucets as possible. It is especially vital to be sure that he does not have immediate access to the hot-water faucet, which could produce a scalding stream that he might be unable to stop.

Generally, children continue to like baths when they have graduated to the regular-size bathtub. For the fairly uncommon youngster who doesn't, but who needs to be cleaned because he crawls or runs about and gets thoroughly grimy, the bath can be made more interesting with boats, rubber balls, and the like, that will float and with which he can entertain himself while you are removing the day's soil from his body.

I urge you not to introduce variety into your youngster's baths via the bubbly detergents that are widely touted, especially around the gift-giving season. Many children are allergic or sensitive to them; each year I see a regular parade of youngsters—raw, red, rashy, itching dreadfully—who are victims of what I call the Post-Christmas Bubble Bath Syndrome. It's true that the bubbling is fun, but I think it is hardly worth the possible price.

There is no particular time of day that is best for bathing a youngster; pick whatever hour is most convenient for you. (It is not a tragedy, either, if you skip a bath for a day or two—if you're just too busy, or traveling, or not feeling well yourself.) Often, parents have found a bath can serve as a great late-afternoon tranquilizer for a child who has refused to take an afternoon nap and has become increasingly cranky and obviously fatigued. If he settles down for a nap at five o'clock, he is liable to snooze through dinner and then be exasperatingly wide awake until midnight or later. A bath at that point seems to relieve tensions, soothe and calm the youngster—but at the same time provide enough stimulation to keep him awake through his evening meal, until his regular bedtime.

Never, ever leave a young child alone in a bathtub, even for an instant—whether to answer the doorbell or telephone, to get a towel from a nearby linen closet, or for any other reason. Drowning ranks third as a cause of death in children under five—and almost half the victims are tots left unattended in the tub. Remember that small children can drown—and have drowned—in two inches of water. And that children left alone in tubs have also been severely scalded and scarred when they took it into their heads to try turning a hot-water tap.

The only safe rule: *if a child is not old enough to bathe himself, he is not old enough to be left alone in the tub.*

How Old Is Old Enough?

Very few children are ready to try bathing themselves before the age of four; most of them aren't ready to do so even then. You'll have to play this a bit by ear. Unless your child has demonstrated a really unusual amount of dexterity and physical coordination, I suggest that even if he asks to bathe himself it's a good idea to defer that step until his fourth birthday. If he is past four, and has not yet brought up the subject himself, you might then suggest the possibility to him.

Before you trust the whole job to a child, conduct some demonstrations for him. Teach him how to handle soap and water, how to get the dirt off, how to rinse himself thoroughly. Then stay with him and watch him do it; there should be several such sessions before you agree to leave him in the tub to bathe himself.

When you first do so, and for some time thereafter, do not disappear to the other end of the house and just let him fend for himself. Leave the bathroom door open, stay within hailing distance, and keep your ears open. Most children take baths pretty noisily. If you cease to hear appropriate sounds and splashes, lose no time in going into the bathroom and finding out why. It is also wise to supervise the child's getting in and out of the tub for weeks, or even months, after he first begins to bathe himself; the getting out is particularly crucial, since careless rinsing—a not uncommon failing among youngsters—can make things extremely slippery.

The Cold or Fever Question

It used to be thought, and still is by many people, that a bath cannot be given if an infant or small child has the sniffles or any other sort of minor illness. That premise was valid, perhaps, in the days before heated homes—and particularly heated bathrooms: the house was freezing during the cold months, and a child who was already sick would be subjected to the additional discomfort of emerging from a warm bath into the icy air.

Now, though, a fever or cold is no reason to forgo a bath
—or a shampoo, either—assuming the room is warm. The
child's hair must, of course, be thoroughly dried before he
goes outdoors in cold weather, whether he's sick or not.
Generally a sick youngster, especially if he's simply been lying
in bed or sitting around coloring or watching TV, doesn't
need a bath desperately; but if he enjoys it, there's no reason
to deny him that pleasure.

As a matter of fact, a bath can even serve a couple of
therapeutic purposes. When a child has fever, one of the
most effective ways to reduce it (assuming he is physically
able to sit up) is to put him in a lukewarm bath and let him
play there for half an hour or so while you splash water over
his shoulders, chest, and back. It will bring down the fever,
because both child and water cool simultaneously. It is a lot
more comfortable for the youngster, and easier for you, than
alcohol sponges, which are sometimes used for the same purpose. And you'll find that if the child has been cranky and
irritable the bathing experience will do a good deal to refresh
him and perk up his spirits.

How About Showers?

I find the question of showers generally comes up fairly
early in the home where both parents are accustomed to
showering and have a definite preference for showers over
tub baths. Actually, any child who can stand up can take a
shower—if he or she wants to. Interestingly, most young children do not like showers. Something about that water cas-
cading down on top of their heads bothers them. They love
to play around lawn sprinklers or hydrants in the summer,
it's true—but the spray in those cases hits the child's body
from the side, rather than in a deluge from above.

If you happen to have a youngster who does evidence a

liking for showers, fine; let him shower. But as with tub baths, you do have to take some safety steps; and it can be a little trickier.

At the start, the child simply should not shower alone. He will need help in setting the right temperature, to begin with. He will need help in turning the water *off*, as well: turning both taps off simultaneously requires a fair amount of strength, as well as dexterity, and if one's turned off before the other, the showerer is left standing under a spray of freezing or scalding water. Further, water temperature in many showers—even if it's "right" at first—does not remain constant throughout the shower, so that occasional readjustment during the shower is necessary. Most children of five cannot manage these things themselves, so a parent should be in the shower at the same time. I think it is preferable for a son to shower with his father, a daughter with her mother.

You will find, if and when you shower with a child, that you are likely to differ on the matter of what is a comfortable temperature and what is not. Adults tend to prefer much hotter baths and showers than children—just because a child's skin is thinner, and an adult has a thicker layer of insulating fat. If you like cooler showers than most adults do, fine. Otherwise, someone's going to have to compromise; I suggest it be you.

As with baths, solo showering for a child should come after careful instruction and supervision, and an adult should be available the first few times—to handle the turning on and off, as well as to rush in and adjust the temperature if the water suddenly turns very hot or very cold (cold won't hurt the child—but extremely hot water can). In summertime, you can make things a lot easier for yourself by limiting a youngster to cold—or very cool—showers; he'll probably like that better anyway.

What if your home—or summer cottage—has no tub at

all, only a shower, and your five-year-old refuses to have anything to do with it? He will probably go along with the family habit in time. Meanwhile, you'll have to sponge-bathe him. Or teach him to clean *himself* that way.

What Is the Sound of One Hand Washing?

As I commented in an earlier chapter, hand washing following a bowel movement is a health necessity, for children and adults alike. Hand washing prior to eating a meal is also a good idea, since germs normally and naturally present on human skin can be mischief-makers in the gastrointestinal tract—and small children, who often do more feeding with their fingers than with utensils, are especially in need of it. Thus it is a good idea for you to wash a child's hands for him at those times, even before he is handling toileting or feeding by himself—just so the idea gets firmly ingrained from the start.

By the time a child reaches the age of two, perhaps even earlier, you might start teaching him to wash his own hands. Take him into the bathroom; have a little step stool at the sink so he can climb up and reach the water. As you wash his hands for him, explain what you're doing; include in your course of instruction the use of a small nailbrush, since grime under fingernails is a good breeding place for infectious organisms. Then gradually introduce him to performing the task himself—at first, as with baths and showers, under your supervision. Go through each step with the child: "Now, Johnny, *you* wash your hands. Here is the soap. Wash the front. Wash the back. You'll have to scrub a little harder to get that smudge off your finger. Now, use the nailbrush. All right, fine. Put the soap back. Now rinse the soap off your hands, and dry them on this towel."

At some point, you will conclude that he is capable of

washing his own hands, and you will direct him to do so. Do not assume that he will perform as efficiently as he did under your tutelage. He will not refuse; most youngsters like water. You are likely to hear a lot of gleeful splashing from the bathroom when you announce that lunch is ready and hand-washing time has arrived. You may also find a river of soapy water seeping out of the bathroom, since what many youngsters seem inclined to do is put in the stopper, fill up the sink, become absorbed in playing with the water, and forget to turn the tap off.

After his session at the sink, it is not at all unusual for a child to show up at the table with one hand scrubbed immaculately, the other bearing all the evidence of his morning spent making mud pies. Do not ask me how this can happen. Obviously, you will send him back to the bathroom to complete the job.

Children are also notoriously inept at drying their hands, even after they have learned to remove the dirt with reasonable efficiency. If the child has come in from outdoor winter play to use the bathroom, then washes his hands as he has been taught but fails to dry them thoroughly, and runs outside again, he is likely to get very chapped hands. So do teach thorough drying too—though that's secondary to the washing in importance.

6

What to Wear, Winter Winds, Summer Sun, and Fresh Air if You Can Find It

I have some fairly strong feelings on what constitutes a sufficient wardrobe for a child—as you will see, and as you might have shrewdly guessed from some comments in the Introduction to this book. If you are well-to-do, and you would like your baby to show off your economic status, I frankly do not feel we are speaking the same language. If, on the other hand, you believe that—whatever your circumstances—you would like your youngster to enjoy life, and you would like the time to enjoy it with him, rather than shopping for clothing, then I urge you to go to as little trouble as possible in clothing him. The time will come soon enough, believe me, when you will be asked to contribute huge sums of money—and possibly long hours as well—in order that your children may maintain themselves to suit their idea of the current mode.

Basics: Bare—or Minimum, Anyway

I suggest you contemplate the thought that the human race has survived for many millennia without going to any special trouble to provide for newborn children, other than assuring that they had a place to sleep, that they had shelter from winter winds and summer sun, and that sustenance was available in some form. Yet I have seen current tomes that solemnly detail dozens of wardrobe items that must be waiting for your child when he enters the world.

The fact of the matter is that there is very little you need buy ahead of time in the way of clothing. Certainly you should not bother to shop for anything elaborate, such as dresses or fancy shirts; people will *give* you dresses or fancy shirts when the child is born—whether you want them or not. No baby *needs* dresses or fancy shirts.

Your newborn baby will need diapers (if he is born in midsummer, and you do not have air conditioning, that, in my opinion, is all he will need at the start). You may plan to use a diaper service, which usually provides you with about a hundred a week—yes, one hundred diapers a week!—to begin with. If you plan to buy and launder your own diapers, I suggest you start with three dozen. (You may assume the diaper services know what they are doing, i.e., that a baby will use perhaps a dozen diapers a day. Which means you can figure on putting a couple of dozen through the wash every two days or so.) Disposable diapers, of course, can be bought as needed.

If you have air conditioning and your baby is born in the summer—or if your baby is born in the winter—you will probably want to put something on the upper part of his body. As a matter of fact, your *baby* will probably feel more comfortable if you do. The something can be a light cotton shirt; half a dozen should be an adequate supply. Make them the kind that close with grippers down front or back or at the shoulders; infants hate having things pulled on and off over their heads.

How about blankets and sleepwear? You may want to have

a receiving blanket—which just means a light cotton blanket that a baby can be softly wrapped in. Some newborn babies seem to enjoy being thus swaddled; some do not. This does not mean that they are ungrateful, just that, from the very start, different people—including babies—have different tastes.

A small baby does not need anything special to sleep in during the summer months. In winter, I personally opt for a very handy invention, the sleeping bag; I suggest you get two or three of them. They are generally made of synthetics and are machine-washable. A sleeping bag has arms that fit tightly at the wrists, but a baglike bottom that lets the baby kick his feet and move around as much as he pleases. It provides excellent insulation. There is no need for a blanket—hence, no worries about the baby's kicking the covers off and waking up with a chill. (Later on, there's something called a sleep suit—a similar garment, serving a similarly useful purpose, that has legs and feet; this will take care of your child's sleeping wardrobe until age five or six. For the cold months, I repeat. A small child doesn't need or want to be heavily covered in warm weather any more than you or I do.) You might want to have one blanket to use for cold-weather carriage trips—but you can use anything you happen to have that will cover the infant, and boots and mittens are unnecessary.

A word—a rather important one—about sleepwear, applying both in infancy and later on. Sleepwear in general has been found to be a frequent source of trouble—meaning severe injury and death—in fires. There are now federal standards governing such garments designed for infants and small children.* As with many such protective regulations, these

* As of mid-1972, regulations required such garments, up to size 6X, to be either flame-retardant or clearly labeled "flammable." This was a "breathing

cannot be taken for granted; some stock, flammable but not so designated, may still remain in stores. Read labels carefully; look for assurance that the garments conform to the federal standards. Hopefully, similar standards will be established in future for other children's clothing, and in larger sizes as well.

That is *it*, so far as the so-called layette is concerned. You might also want to have a couple of pairs of plastic or other waterproof panties for protection on special occasions. But I really feel that a newborn baby—any baby, in fact, who spends all his time in crib, carriage, and playpen, and is not yet coming into active encounter with the environment—really does not need anything else.

(If close friends and family insist upon bestowing new-baby gifts upon you in the form of clothing, and do not think that diapers make a suitably festive present, I suggest you prevail upon them to be of real help, and provide whatever pretty little things they like—*in size 3 and up*. It will be nice to have them instantly available, when you really do need to buy your child clothes. When you are talking with these people, use a lot of terms like "machine-washable," "no-iron," and—if skirts or dresses are contemplated—"permanent pleats.")

You do not need to hand-wash an infant's diapers, shirts, or any other clothing—but I do advise you to use soap in your machine, rather than detergent, for the baby's things, until he's crawling and really gets them dirty; detergents can often cause skin irritation, and it's best not to take chances. When the clothes really get grimy, use detergent to get the dirt out, but then run them through a full cycle again in plain water; that way, you'll be certain that all detergent residue

---

period" for the manufacturers, presumably to permit old stock to be moved out; as of July 29, 1973, there is a complete ban on flammable sleepwear in these sizes.

has been removed. The skin of most preschool children is sufficiently delicate to need this protection.

Once a baby has begun to crawl, it's kind to give his little body a bit more protection than simply diapers. Shirts and overalls, which many parents like, are fine—but get overalls that snap open from the bottom; otherwise you will have to go through the entire undressing-and-dressing hassle every time a diaper needs to be changed. Stretch suits are also great: they snap up the front and down the legs, they go over the baby's feet for extra protection, and they are a very good buy *because* they are stretchable; usually, a stretch suit will wear out before it's outgrown—which means you will not be left with a pile of perfectly good clothing that can't be used because it doesn't fit any more.

When your child has begun to take himself to the toilet or potty seat, it will be helpful to abandon head-to-toe outfits and provide pants with elastic tops; children can usually learn to manage the simple pulling down pretty easily, while snaps, buttons, or other fasteners are likely to stump them at this stage.

One other comment on general wardrobe. I have never seen any need for a child to wear an undershirt under whatever else he is wearing—and no parent of an undershirted child has ever been able to explain to me why his or her child was wearing one. It may be that one of these years some exhaustive study will demonstrate that small children who wear undershirts get fewer colds or hangnails, or grow taller, or read earlier, than children who do not. I have observed no such difference in my own practice, nor has any other pediatrician I know. So far as we now know, undershirts represent extra laundry. Period. Remember the premise of this book. I urge you to omit them from your child's wardrobe.

Baby, It's Cold Outside—
So How Come You've Got Prickly Heat?

Probably the most common clothing mistake young parents make, so far as I have observed, is to *overdress* their babies. Perhaps the prevalent overprotectiveness revolves around the feeling that young children are somehow less able to cope than older folks. It's perfectly true that a newborn baby has just emerged from a body-temperature environment. He adapts very quickly, however—practically instantly. Otherwise delivery rooms would have to be kept at 97°, wouldn't they? Or else we would all have built-in pouches, like kangaroos.

In fact, your newborn child's temperature-maintenance mechanism goes into operation immediately—a mechanism that maintains his internal temperature no matter what the temperature of the surrounding air, one that is not quite as efficient as yours and mine, but will be within a few months.

Dress your baby as lightly as the temperature permits. If he is too cold, he will let you know about it; the discomfort of being too cold is one of the few things an infant cannot adjust to. He will let you know by crying loudly; if he is bawling and his skin is also sort of mottled-looking, he is *very* cold. Babies are not likely to complain if they are too *hot*, however; they will just lie there and sweat, and if multiple layers of clothing have blocked their sweat glands, they are quite likely to get prickly heat—even in the dead of winter. And don't try vainly to get a child's hands and feet just as warm as the rest of him; they are not meant to be.

As I said, a carriaged baby needs only a blanket or some other warm covering when he is wheeled outdoors in the winter. Children old enough and mobile enough to play outdoors in the cold and snow do, of course, need extra protection.

But again, don't overdo it. Few sights are quite so pathetic as a tiny figure lumbering stiffly into view like a miniature moon-walker, crying in a small, helpless voice, "Mommy, bend me!" Choose sturdy, *wind-repellent* snowsuit materials, light in weight. Put just one sweater underneath. That's enough; it will give the child plenty of protection from the cold—while maintaining room to move.

Need such a youngster wear a hat? Not necessarily. Small children detest hats that are forced upon them when they're not really needed; most children's heads sweat a great deal, and the hat can become decidedly uncomfortable. Force a hat on your child only if it's cold enough for *you* to need one.

Small children seem to have even less need for gloves and mittens than older folks do. I'm not sure why; perhaps it's because they are generally running about when they are out-doors, and have less time to think about the fact that their fingers are turning blue. Which they might—but no one, believe me, has ever been oblivious to incipient frostbite, and your child will not be either.

I would say that it is a good idea to send a youngster out to play in the snow wearing gloves or mittens, preferably the latter. He will probably shed them. You do not want to have to buy a new pair every couple of weeks; and if he sits down to rest, he may become aware that his hands are cold (many children don't feel the need of hand covering even then, strangely enough). For those reasons, it is a good idea to attach the mittens to the ends of his sleeves. Safety pins don't work particularly well; there's not enough maneuverability in case he should *want* to get them on again. A short length of elastic is probably the best bet.

Lined, lightweight boots are the footwear of choice in cold weather.

For Want of a Shoe

I have had parents bring babies to my office fully shod at the age of six months. Somehow, I have discovered, they have got the notion—a mistaken one—that forcing a child's feet into shoes will benefit them in some way. I suspect that such a notion is not discouraged by manufacturers of small shoes.

The fact is that there is no real need to put shoes on a child until he is ready to walk *outside*. Walking around your house without shoes will not hurt a child. It is, in fact, good for him. As is outdoor walking on sand or grass. Going barefoot provides excellent foot-muscle development and exercise. His ankles will not fall apart; always bear in mind the fact that he was not born with shoes and that they are strictly a human invention.

Shoes do play a necessary role when a child begins to walk on surfaces that may injure him. Every human society has indeed developed footwear of some sort for protective purposes. (*Not supportive* purposes.) On the street, or on other surfaces that may actually injure the feet—a beach littered with sharp shell fragments, for instance, or a badly splintered floor—your child should have shoes.

"Even" inexpensive shoes are acceptable, notes a leading child-care guide. I would go further. Do buy inexpensive shoes. Sneakers or something similar—soft shoes, with rubber soles—are your best bet. (I am astonished by children who manage to walk in stiff, high shoes; I am also in awe of parents who have the patience and strength to get them on their children's feet.) Buy the cheapest pair that fits; they're likely to be quickly outgrown, and why should you pay a premium price for something that is not going to last very long? Nor is it a good idea, in case you've thought of it, to buy shoes a couple of sizes too large. How would *you* like to struggle around in shoes two sizes too large for you?

When you go to buy your child a pair of shoes, take him with you; nothing is as dependable as the child's own feet in determining size. Chances are the shoe salesman will have some suggestions. Ignore them. Once the shoes are on the child's feet—both feet—have him stand up. There should be half an inch of space beyond his big toe. (If you cannot *feel* his big toe, the shoe is too hard.) If there is less, you need a larger size. If there is substantially more—especially if the heel of the shoe flops up and down when the child walks or runs (have him walk and run, *in the store*)—you need a smaller size.

If you do not spend a great deal of money on shoes for your child, you will be willing to buy shoes more often, and your child will be fitted properly as his feet grow.

A *Rule Upon Which to Fall Back*

Dress your child as you would dress yourself if it were socially acceptable to do so. *Corollary Rule:* Make allowances for your personal hangups. If you are always chillier than other people, for example, put one less layer of clothing on your child than your own gut feelings would lead you to put on yourself.

"Well, Don't Just Stand There—Put Your Clothes On!"

Do not expect your twenty-two-month-old to dress himself —even if he has an astonishingly large vocabulary, is walking competently by himself, and seems capable of all kinds of abstract thought. Self-dressing typically does not even *begin* —"begin" means some kind of gingerly attempt—until the age of two years, and the child who is fully capable of getting all his clothes on by himself under the age of four years is rare. As a matter of fact, he is unlikely to master some of the intricacies before the age of six.

Each child is different, and when it comes to putting on clothes, a number of different skills are involved. Thus, there are no hard-and-fast guidelines. Most children find socks the easiest procedure to learn first; there are no fasteners involved, and the sock is also conveniently shaped: it offers instant clues to the novice puller-on-er. Pull-on pants with elastic waistbands are also usually fairly easy to learn. Both those and shirts have labels, and it is a happy and consistent coincidence that the labels are always on the inside back— so that label position is a good clue for the young learner. Buttons, by the way, are easier for children to learn to cope with than snap grippers, since the latter require strength.

The last dressing skill children generally learn is shoelace tying. Don't expect that capability to develop much before the age of six. And in general, girls are a little more adept at learning dressing skills than boys.

If He Weighs Eight Pounds, and the Thermometer Says 60°, Do You Divide by the Wind Chill Factor?

In the matter of exposing your baby to the elements, I urge you—as in a number of other areas—to (a) make things easy for yourself and (b) avoid wasting time with either old wives' tales or pseudoscientific gobbledygook for which no sane reasoning exists. Indoors or outdoors, you will then have more time to spend discoursing with your child, whether about the weather or anything else that interests both of you.

As I pointed out earlier, babies do not need to be kept in hothouses. They are not orchids. They are people like you and me, and they have internal temperature controls just as you and I do. This is true no matter how much they weigh and whatever their ages (assuming they did not arrive prematurely—in which case everything I have said, and will say, applies once they have achieved normal weight and your doctor has pronounced the child's development at least equal to that of a full-term infant).

Cold weather, in short, is no more dangerous to a tiny infant, let alone a three-year-old, than it is to anyone else. Naturally, the child should be dressed appropriately for the weather—just as you would wear a heavy coat, and not a bikini or swimming trunks, in the middle of winter. But—as I warned earlier—do not *over*dress your child. Reread those warnings.

I hope you will thus be encouraged to ignore the advice rampant in some quarters—and in some child-care books— that hint of complex calculations involving the child's weight and degrees Fahrenheit. I have before me two such books. One offers a formula which would unerringly arrive at the conclusion that an eight-pound baby must be kept indoors when the temperature outside is less than 63° F. The other states in so many words that it is perfectly all right for an eight-pound baby to be taken out if the thermometer reads 60°. *I* would say that your eight-pound baby may be taken out whatever the temperature, if you feel that you wish to take him somewhere and your own doctor has not issued instructions to the contrary for some reason. If you do not wish to take him out, there is of course no reason why you must. The air in your house is probably better for him than the stuff that is drifting around outside; upon which, more comment shortly.

Just one more myth-dispelling note about winter. Neither cold nor dampness causes colds or other upper respiratory infections. Colds are caused by viruses—at least 113 different viruses, at last count, according to researchers at the National Institutes of Health. Controlled studies have clearly shown that neither drafts nor dampness increase an individual's susceptibility to colds. Nor do folks get more colds during the winter months because the blustery winds whip the nasty germs about—despite the statements you may have heard (and which I have read more times than I care to count). People do, it is true, get more colds in winter, statistically speaking; they get them from *other people*, with whom they are wont to spend longer hours enclosed indoors than in the summer months.

So when you take your child out in the wintertime, it is a good idea not to take him to crowded public places, if colds-prevention is what you have in mind.

Summer Is Something Else Again

While cold weather isn't a special threat to your child, strong sun and/or high heat can be, and he needs protection from both. The younger he is, the greater protection he needs. This is because—although his thermostat is working perfectly well—two other safeguards are not fully operative at the start.

One of these is sweat glands. Small babies' simply do not work very efficiently at first, and that is why they get prickly heat when they are overdressed and put in a hot, humid place; for the same reason, they are more liable to heat stroke (sometimes inaccurately called sunstroke)—which involves dangerous increases in internal temperature and is a very serious matter.

The other is the child's skin itself. It is thinner than yours. And whatever its color, it has not had a chance to build up protection against burning; the lighter it is (though light eyes are often a better clue to sun-sensitivity), the more susceptible it is to burning—but it is important to remember that even the darkest-skinned baby *can* be burned by the sun. Sunburn is a miserable experience, as you know if you have had it. It is kind to protect your child from it.

As you can probably guess, air conditioning is a perfectly fine thing for your baby. Newborn nurseries, in fact, are now air-conditioned, the temperature maintained at approximately 70° to 72°F. (21°or 22°C.). They were not always, and when atmospheric temperatures soared to the nineties, fevers of 106° were not unusual.

If it is hot and humid enough outside for you to be decidedly uncomfortable, it is too hot for an infant; he will be better off indoors, in the presence of air conditioning, or at least a fan to draw off perspiration from his body.

So far as the sun goes—again, ignore any poundage correlations you may see elsewhere—the most dangerous period by far is the four-hour period from about 10:00 A.M. to about 2:00 P.M., when the sun is high in the sky, its rays more intense. Haze or overcast does not diminish the danger. Place as well as time is pertinent: any situation in which glare is reflected—as from snow, beach, water—increases the effect.

Infants should be exposed to direct sunlight only for periods of five or ten minutes to start—and not during that dangerous midday period. A child with very light hair and/or eyes should be kept out of direct sunlight entirely until he is a year or two old; again, a reminder that eye color is sometimes your best guideline—although redheads are extremely susceptible to sunburn *whatever* the color of their eyes.

After that age, you should still be extremely careful in exposing small children to the sun; very pale or light-eyed ones should be kept completely out of that midday sun, period.

Sun-screening preparations are fine—if they are, in fact, sun screens. Read the label carefully. They should contain a screening agent that filters out the sun's burning rays, and "promotes tan" does not necessarily mean "prevents burn"— although a product *may* do both. Such products need not be oily or sticky, and in fact it is a good idea to get one that isn't, especially for the beach, since sand can stick to, and irritate, skin coated with a layer of goo. The sticky ones are sticky because the manufacturer hopes that they will not wash off in swimming; this is a nice thought, but the effort is not effective, and any sunburn preventive, sticky or not, must be reapplied after swimming. Pre-Sun and Sun Sports Lotion are two of the several effective non-sticky preparations.

Never use an oil—even a so-called "baby oil"—to protect your child or anyone else against sunburn. Oil, remember, is used for frying.

Other protective devices against sun and heat may also be helpful at appropriate ages. A beach umbrella, for one—but don't get a false sense of security; sand and water reflect the sun onto those beneath the umbrella, and the reflected glare, if it goes on long enough, is sufficient to burn a baby's skin. A sun hat is also useful for a toddler whose hair is light and thin (a thick, dark head of hair provides enough protection); choose white or a light color.

How about sunglasses? Fine, if a youngster finds the sunlight uncomfortable. Typically, a dark-eyed child rarely complains or asks for dark glasses. A child with gray, green, blue, or hazel eyes may be quite uncomfortable in the sun, though, and may tell you so if he is articulate enough; or he may demonstrate his discomfort by squinting and covering his eyes when he is out in the sun. Just make sure, if you get dark glasses for your child, that they are of good quality and that there are no visual distortions; a tot has a hard enough time getting around, without having to negotiate the hills and valleys that often appear underfoot when the ground is viewed through distorted sunglass lenses.

Children who like the comfort of dark glasses, I have found, are unlikely to lose or drop them. Sometimes, though, an active youngster does have trouble; there are elastic bands you can buy to keep them on.

All of the foregoing precautions apply to a child who is an albino—one who has no protective pigment in his skin and eyes. If possible, keep such a child out of the sun entirely.

There is one final risk involving sunlight—one that applies to people of any age. Certain medications—prominently the group of antibiotics called tetracyclines and the phenothiazines (the latter are a group of potent tranquilizers rarely prescribed for children)—can increase susceptibility to sunburn, heat problems, or both. If your youngster is under any medication whatever, this question should be discussed with your doctor.

"Where Did You Go?" "Out."
"What Did You Do?" "Breathe."

As we all know, the air out there is just about anything but fresh. It's not really within the purview of this book to sound additional broad alarms on the subject. Nor do I suggest that you send your youngster out to play wearing a gas mask—unless, of course, you and the rest of the family view it as necessary for yourselves.

There are, however, a couple of problems peculiar to the preschooler vis-à-vis the pollution menace.

If your child has a history of allergy, especially allergy of a respiratory nature, and you live in an urban area, he is likely to be more comfortable indoors when there is an atmospheric inversion situation, intensifying the smog. An air-purifier or -conditioner will be helpful.

If yours is a rural area, bear in mind the toxic effects of crop pesticides. Ideally, they should be applied in still-air conditions, with due consideration of their potential for drifting into human habitats. In fact, they are often *not* so applied. Pesticides can make people sick, and even kill; their risk is roughly inversely proportional to body weight. I.e., the smaller the victim, the more critical the effects. If farmers in your neighborhood are spraying pesticides indiscriminately, I urge you to do something about it, on behalf of your child.

Finally, this ominous note. Lead poisoning, as most of us know, results from a child's eating paint and plaster. Not all of us know that it can also come—slowly and cumulatively —from breathing sufficient exhausts of vehicles powered by leaded gasoline. There is strong indication, at this writing, that leaded gasoline can release enough of the substance into the nearby atmosphere to create dangerous concentrations —not especially dangerous for adults, or even for older children, but for those small children whose height brings them close to the exhaust-discharge level. A report by the Federal Environmental Protection Administration has calculated that a child's swallowing ten teaspoonfuls of dust within a hundred feet of a busy roadway over an eight-month period would probably become a victim of lead poisoning. That "busy roadway," testing in many areas has made clear, might be a turnpike—or a heavily trafficked city street.

Obviously, it is good to (a) see that your small child does not stroll on foot along, or play near, streets or roads frequented by a great deal of automotive traffic; and (b) join and encourage any community or other efforts to diminish automotive lead pollution of the atmosphere. If you suspect that your child may have been exposed to such hazards, consult your physician or your local health department.

7

Law and Order for Beginners
and How to Enforce It
(Remember Who's in Charge Here!)

I find that a certain amount of terror suddenly seizes new parents—it usually happens when the baby is about a month old—with the sudden realization that this is a Human Being they have on their hands: that they will not only have to feed, clothe, and tend to the other physical needs of this human being but somehow *teach* him or her how to get along in this world. There quickly ensues an anxious scanning of newspaper articles (somehow the phrase "delinquent" leaps out of every paragraph) and a mental review of all the "difficult" children they have known (often not excluding themselves).

Let me assure you that with some basic understanding—which I hope to present in this chapter—you will very probably be perfectly adequate to the task of acquainting your child with the necessary rules of behavior. And that you have more time to mull it over than you might suppose. Let us begin at the beginning.

He Just Lies There—But What Is He Plotting?

I recall a science fiction story I once read that described a newborn child who spent all his waking hours planning a coup that would establish him as the undisputed dictator of the household (I cannot recall the title or the author, and please don't write and remind me unless you *are* the author). The details are a bit hazy, but if I remember correctly, by the end of the tale the tot had gradually accomplished his purpose, his parents had actually been done in by his nefarious schemes, and he was about to be adopted by some other innocent victim. It was entertaining, but it *was* fiction. A new baby, in fact, is totally incapable of basic logical thinking, let alone complex ideas involving future time.

Yet it happens again and again. You bring your new baby home from the hospital, you have visitors a few days later, you hear Johnny crying in his room, you excuse yourself, you prepare to go and comfort him, and invariably someone will cry in shocked tones, "You're not going in to pick him up, are you? You'll spoil him!"

This is nonsense, and I suggest you ignore these people; they are wrong. Johnny is crying because he is in some way uncomfortable, and your going in to comfort him will in no way damage his little psyche. On the contrary, it will reassure and strengthen him.

There is just no way to "spoil" a child during the first few months of his or her life. I would advise you to follow your own instincts when it comes to responding to your baby's cries. Very few parents can bear to listen to loud, long crying without taking some action; as many parents have put it, they "get all knotted up inside." Normally and naturally, they rush in and try to comfort the child in whatever way they can. Which results in indulging the baby's every whim during those first few months—feeding him when he's hungry, changing him when he's wet, letting him sleep when he's tired, playing with him when he wants to be played with, moving him about when he seems bored, and so on. It will not harm the baby one little bit, since he is totally dependent upon you at this stage. No one who is completely powerless to answer his own basic needs is in a position to manipulate others.

This doesn't mean, of course, that you need instantly drop what you are doing every time the baby cries. You may, of course, want to, for one reason or another: "Oh dear, Daphne's crying and that means she needs to be fed" will cut off your friend's telephone tirade very neatly. Or you may run into Daphne's room, and let the toast burn, because you are genuinely convinced that Daphne is in some sort of serious trouble.

But if you are in the den trying desperately to balance the checkbook, and what Daphne wants is entertainment, you really don't have to abandon your activity and spend the rest of the afternoon playing with her. To a baby, anything new is entertaining, and it is quite possible that Daphne is just tired of lying there and staring at the same wallpaper or the same rag doll. You might turn her over or give her a different toy—or, if it's human company she craves, put her in her playpen or infant seat, put the pen or seat in the den, and let her watch *you* for a while.

You are probably wondering, at this point, just how you are going to know what it is your baby wants when he or she cries. Is it milk, or water, or a clean diaper, or playing, or cuddling, or a change of scene, or relief from an agonizing pain, or what? You *won't* know the very first day the baby's home—and of course, until you do, you'll check all possibilities. But you will know very soon after that (most of the time, anyway), within a matter of days, a week or two at most.

Not because there is some mysterious genetic mechanism at work. Anyone who spends a good deal of time with a particular baby—mother, father, sibling, nursemaid, even a frequent baby-sitter—develops this ability. Strangers won't know, though, and if they do not have children of their own, they will be very mystified by this seeming telepathy. They will be visiting you and hear one-month-old Michael cry. If you remark, "Uh-oh, he just had another bowel movement, and he wants to be changed," they will be amazed when you go into Michael's room to look and, by gum, you were right!

There is one kind of crying some (not all) infants do that doesn't fit into any of the categories I've mentioned. If you have just put Karen to bed, and within a couple of minutes after you've tucked her in you begin to hear a sort of plaintive moaning cry—no matter how it tugs at your heartstrings, I advise you to wait a few minutes.

Karen may be one of those babies who need to "crank" for a little while before they fall asleep. If you dash into her room and pick her up, she'll immediately wake up fully, she'll stop crying, you'll then put her back in her crib—now a little *more* tired—and it will start all over again and go on even longer; repeat the process a few times, and you and Karen will both end up totally exhausted. So start by giving her that few minutes. If she really needs you desperately for any reason, the cry will change; it will become loud, strong, and persistent, and should of course be answered promptly. But if she is simply going "Aaaanhh, aaaanhh, aaaanhh," intermittently, you can ignore it.

During these first months you will, by and large, have done a good deal of accommodating to the baby, making every effort to determine your child's needs and to fulfill them as promptly as possible. You will be delighted to learn that it gets easier and easier. You will not only learn to readily discern the different sounds he uses to make his various needs known. You will also discover that by the time he is about three months old he can stand a bit of frustration: he can wait a little longer to be fed, he can put up with his dirty diaper for a few more minutes, and so on. You can adjust his schedule, here and there, to be a bit more agreeable to yours. This is his first clue that he is not, actually, the center of the world.

He's Getting Around Now (or, Why Is This Child Suicidal?)

As soon as your baby reaches the stage of mobility, whether on two feet or four, you will have to start instituting some rules. These first rules are for one purpose, primarily: to protect the child from himself. Take my word for it: mobile babies will put themselves in all sorts of dangerous positions.

They are old enough to move around and curious enough to explore their immediate environment. They are *not* old enough to protect themselves from potentially tragic accidents. The main reason is that they just don't know any better. A second operative factor is that small children often do not respond the way adults do to what you and I would consider noxious stimuli. A third is that they are not physically equipped to haul themselves out of danger, even when that danger is recognized (the smallest tots, for example, are instinctively afraid of heights—but their muscles are not sufficiently responsive to prevent their falling). A fourth is the child's size per se: toxic substances are invariably more toxic, the smaller the individual.

I will not subject you to tales of the terrible disasters I have had occasion to deal with. But please believe that the word "*No!*"—complete with exclamation point—really must become part of your vocabulary now. It is necessary to prevent your child's falling out of the sixteenth-story window, setting himself on fire, gulping down poisons, and more. As he becomes more adept at getting into things, the number of negatives will have to increase—until they sink in. You may also feel, somewhere along the line, that you need track shoes.

Year-old tots are not logical beings—not, at least, in any sense that you can grasp. This is a fact, and it can prove extremely frustrating. When Charles has reached the crawling stage and is heading for the hot radiator for the umpteenth time, you may begin to feel that Charles is a bit retarded when he repeatedly ignores your command to "Get *away* from there!" He is not. Any normal child will ignore you— until he has been injured. (What does "You'll get burned" mean if he's never *been* burned?) You do not want him to learn the hard way, of course. So you will keep your eyes open, and you will—when you see that he ignores your warnings—grab him by the scruff of the neck and forcibly remove him from danger.

Someday he will surprise you. He will start to do what he has repeatedly been told not to do, but he will approach the forbidden area slyly, looking back over his shoulder. He is beginning to get the idea. Something has penetrated. Eureka. I'll pick up from that point a little later. In the meantime, your child must be protected if he is not to do himself in. The moment your child has the freedom of the house it is time for *babyproofing*. This is a process that may be a nuisance at first; you do have to sit down and give it some thought. But once you have done so, it is going to make life a lot safer for your child—and a lot easier for you. Parental relaxation and peace of mind are things I am very much in favor of.

For the first and only time in this book, I am going to present a set of directives. I have seen too many heartbreaking accidents involving children in this age group—and nation-wide statistics clearly indicate that my experience is far from unique—*not* to do so. Children under five account for staggering proportions of accidents in our country (at this age, in fact, accidents account for far more deaths than disease); three quarters of such mishaps, whether fatal or not, occur in the home. Virtually all of them are preventable.

The list that follows singles out the major sources of danger. Please also note the precautions about bathing (pages 78–83) and showering (pages 84–85), as well as the comments on paints (page 72), pets and toys (Chapter 9), and sleepwear (pages 90–91).

- *Keep anything that might be eaten, and should not be, under lock and key.* This includes all medications of whatever nature (meaning aspirin and vitamins, as well as obviously dangerous items such as narcotics); if a child is helping himself to medications, there is no one controlling the dosage. An amount of aspirin that would merely make an adult sick could kill a toddler. It also includes absolutely anything that is eatable or drinkable (unfortunately, toddlers are not turned off by repellent odors—a fact that has been established in research), including: floor waxes, detergents, furniture polish, pesticides of any and all kinds, paints and other household-crafts liquids. Medicine cabinets, under-the-sink cabinets, and utility closets should be inaccessible.
- *Get small objects out of the way.* By these I mean anything that is small enough to be put in a child's mouth and might conceivably either block the child's windpipe or cause direct damage if it's swallowed. Included: pins and needles, nails and screws, thumbtacks, small pieces of jewelry, hairpins, small toys belonging to older siblings.
- *Beware of sharp instruments.* Don't expect a small child to know the dangerous, business end of a knife or nail clipper from the other. Like medications and small swallowable objects, sharp instruments should be inaccessible to your crawler or toddler. Check out all areas of your home; this admonition includes kitchen implements, manicure para-

phernalia, workshop or craft tools, yard and gardening implements.

• *Tots and matches don't mix.* Or any other sources of flame or fire. Keep matches, lighters, lighter fluids out of reach. See that the child stays far from the stove (and when you're cooking, turn pot handles away from the edge, so curious hands can't reach up and pull over boiling liquids). Never leave the child alone in a room with a lighted stove, fire, candle, or oil lamp.

• *Eliminate electrical hazards within your child's reach.* Keep electric cords far from crib and playpen; they are marvelous things to chew on and can cause rather horrible electrical burns. Plug up all unused outlets (by securely taping them with heavy tape, or by using the blanks you can buy at hardware stores); a hairpin or other small metal object poked into an outlet can result in electrocution.

• *Keep guns unloaded.* And store the ammunition under lock and key.

• *Screen visitors to your home.* While you may have removed all dangerous objects from your child's reach, new ones may enter via visitors' purses and pockets, which may contain such attractive perils as potent medicines, pocket knives, nail files, etc. Coats should not be hung where the child can reach the pockets, or handbags left out of sight (e.g., in a bedroom).

• *Guard your youngster from falls.* All windows—even those just a few feet from the ground, but most particularly those on higher floors—should be securely screened or barred. If you've more than one floor, all stairs should be securely gated top and bottom, the gates used from the moment the child begins to crawl until he can capably negotiate stairs by himself.

• *And then look around for other possible hazards.* Get down to child level—literally and figuratively—and see what else could conceivably prove a danger, based on the character of your particular home. Do you, for example, have venetian blinds? Cut open the cord loops, which can strangle if small heads are put through them. Have you a yard? Fence it—to keep your child in, wandering animals out. Do you do your laundry in an old-fashioned wringer washer? Spend a few dollars for an automatic safety release, so your son or daughter won't be one of the tens of thousands of toddlers whose hands and arms are mangled each year. Does your dry cleaner deliver the clothes plastic-wrapped? Hand the wrappings back at the door, or destroy them promptly; many a youngster has been suffocated in innocent play with these clinging plastics.

Finally—and I cannot emphasize this too much—keep an eye on your youngster at all times; know where he is and what he is doing. And never underestimate either his curiosity or, once he is on his feet, his agility—his ability to climb to the top shelves of bookcases and cabinets, for instance.

Permission vs. Permissive

Placing restrictions upon a child primarily to preserve his life and limbs is just the first stage of what—for lack of a better term—I will refer to as *discipline*. Never mind the dictionary definitions of this word. What *I* mean by it is: establishing and enforcing a set of rules to which you expect your child to adhere, in order to make of him or her a civilized creature with whom both you and others will be able to live. It is not to be confused with *punishment*, a last-ditch resort that follows absolute refusal to conform to the rules, and of which I shall speak separately later. Nor does it mean making him or her some sort of silent slave who can come to no individual decisions; discipline in the preschool years is in fact necessary in order to develop the ability for later decision-making—and moreover, your child wants and seeks it.

For some twenty or twenty-five years people raised their children by a theory loosely termed "permissiveness." By this was meant, they believed, refraining from inhibiting the child's individual development; the method was setting down no rules for the child to follow, so far as behavior was concerned. Anything the little darling wanted to do was perfectly fine; no matter how annoying or distasteful to others, it was "self-expression."

Many of these children—some of them have made headlines, and not because of great artistic or scientific achievement—grew up very confused. Far from feeling free and confident, they tended to emerge into adult life with a strong sense of insecurity, of being unloved and uncared for. Why? Simply because discipline is part of a parent's expression of love for the child. It is a way of saying, "I care whether or not you will be able to get along in this world," that you want the child to be prepared to deal with people and things he or she will encounter later on, when you are not around to promulgate guidelines.

This takes place on a subconscious level. You are not going to get instant obedience by announcing, "I am telling you to wash your hands because I love you, and I do not want you to get germs in your mouth, and also, when you are twenty, you will thank me, because people will invite you to their dinner tables and not shun you because your hands are always grimy." A four-year-old cannot think that far ahead and is likely to respond with, "If you love me, you'll let me eat with dirty hands, because that's what I want to do." You do not deal with a four-year-old this way. The hands must be washed because you say so, and that's that, no matter the protests. Underneath it all, whatever the fondness for dirty hands, *your guidance is wanted.*

Children will very often "test" their parents by announcing plans to do something that is potentially dangerous. Freddy—who has never before climbed a tree—might, for example, come up to you and say, "Daddy, I am going to go out and climb to the top of that big tree."

If Daddy's answer, based on the mistaken notion that he is freeing Freddy to express himself, is, "That's fine—go right ahead," Freddy is going to be terrified. He has committed himself to climbing the tree and feels bound to do so, since you have made no effort to stop him—despite the fact that you both know he is not capable of performing the feat safely. Yet no one seems anxious to protect him. The real message of Freddy's question was: "I would like to climb that tree, Daddy, but I want you to tell me I may not do so because I might get badly hurt, and you don't want me to take that chance because you love me very much."

I have seen children do *non*dangerous testing as well. I recall, when I was in medical school, visiting the home of another student who had a small child and was proud of using "permissive" methods of upbringing. As my husband and I chatted with our hosts, four-and-a-half-year-old Billy entered the room and helped himself to a peach from a bowl on the table around which we were sitting. After taking one bite, he returned the peach to the bowl and selected a pear—with which he did precisely the same thing. He proceeded to repeat this performance with half the fruit in the bowl—importantly, glancing at his parents as he put back each piece. He was totally ignored. And—though of course I said nothing —I was horrified. Billy's repetition of what he sensed was unacceptable behavior, like Freddy's announcement, was a plea for some indication that his parents cared enough about him to provide guidance.

Discipline, in short, is a necessity. It is part of your job as a parent to put forth rules about correct and incorrect behavior, to provide your child with a concept of what is expected of him, to point out what is permitted and what is not acceptable. Based, of course, not on what your friends, your relatives, your neighbors, or I consider proper, but upon your feelings and attitudes about how you want your child to behave.

Clarity Begins at Home

Children instinctively want the approval of their parents. This does not mean that your child will instantly grasp and follow all your instructions, even when you have repeated them ten or twenty times. But it does mean that you will be able to count on *eventual* cooperation. That assurance will, I hope, sustain you through what may be some irritating experiences from the approximate age of two years onward. Which is when a child usually begins to realize that he is a distinct individual and is eager to find out what he can get away with. He will try whatever he can think of.

You will spare yourself a good many tiresome and unpleasant hassles if you remember this basic: whatever rules of behavior you set forth should be *clear and consistent*.

By the latter, I mean consistent both from day to day and from one parent to the other. Anything else is going to confuse the child; he will not be sure what you expect, and you cannot hope to get the response you want. If Johnny is not allowed to play with the contents of the wastebasket on Tuesday, he shouldn't be permitted to do so on Thursday either. If Mommy thinks it's cute that Marcia scribbles all over the weekly news magazine, Marcia is not going to understand why Daddy seems to be having a fit about it. You must present a united front. If you have a disagreement about a house rule, don't air it in front of the child; discuss it quietly between you, come to an agreement or compromise, and stick by it.

This agreement between the parents is vital—since, when a child gets old enough, he will attempt to play off one parent against the other. If he finds that he can wheedle certain things out of his father and others out of his mother, when the other parent would have said no, there are going to be hard feelings all around—between you and your child, and between you and your spouse as well.

Another habit that will avoid aggravation is simply thinking before you answer a child's question. If Michael asks, "May I go in the bathroom and play with my sailboat?" don't just absent-mindedly say yes and then change your mind thirty seconds later when you realize that you are expecting company and Michael's seafaring invariably results in slopping up the entire bathroom and there will not be time to clean it before your visitors arrive. By the time you think of this Michael will already be running the water in the tub and will burst into tears when you rush in and call a halt. By the same token, if your answer is initially no—for whatever reasons—*be prepared to stick to it*, through whatever flak you get from the child.

Should you give a child reasons for your answers or directives? I think that in general you should—assuming it is a reason the child can understand and that you have time under the particular circumstances. "Get away from the stove this minute!" should not need any lengthy discussion—not just then, at any rate. But by and large it is helpful—to both you and the child—if he can get some idea of cause and effect, and of the logic behind things, since he will eventually have to make his own choices and think things out for himself.

Sometimes, of course, your reasoning is simply too complex for a child to grasp, and in those cases "Because I say so" will just have to do; you are bigger than he is, and you are in charge, after all. But in many instances it's easy to offer an explanation. If Susie asks, "May I have a cooky?" and you know very well it will spoil her appetite, "No, because we're going to eat supper soon" is preferable to just plain "No."

Usually children will happily accept logical explanations. I remember one incident from my own childhood. I was five, and was just being permitted to cross our street—which was a one-way street—alone. "Remember," my father warned me, "you always have to look both ways before you cross." I asked, "Why? It's a one-way street!" My father, who had the patience of two thousand saints, replied, "Because every now and then a car makes a mistake and goes the wrong way." Okay, that made sense. I did look both ways. I was probably the only child on the block who did. And one day, sure enough, a car came down the street the wrong way. Which confirmed my faith in my father's omniscience.

Bear in mind that small children are extremely literal. Say what you mean, and say it precisely. If, for example, you and I were talking in my office, and I had to take care of another patient, I might say to you, "Would you like to go out and sit in the waiting room while I look at Eddie's throat, and we'll continue our talk later?" You would say, "Certainly," because you would know that what I really meant was, "Please go out and sit in the waiting room."

A child, however, will take the question literally. So that if you are visiting at someone's house, and you turn to Michael and say, "Shall we leave now?" don't be surprised if he says flatly, "No." You are going to look like a fool if you then say, "Well, we're leaving." If you didn't want him to decide, you shouldn't have asked him in the first place. Of course if it really doesn't matter to you whether you leave at that moment or not, ask him if you like; but then abide by his decision.

Giving a child an indefinite choice is another trap of which to beware. If Michael is asked, "What would you like to wear today?" you're going to be very annoyed when he declares that he would like to wear his red velvet suit to go play in the sandbox. Of course you will say no. But that's not logical, is it? Same thing as the "Shall we leave now?" question. If you want to offer him a choice—about what to wear, what to eat, what game to play, or anything else—narrow it down: "Which would you like to wear—your red overalls or your blue overalls?"

There are going to be times when, no matter how sweet and reasonable you are, you are not going to get any cooperation. I think you have to play each situation by ear and key your reactions, basically, to *your* needs and the demands of the moment.

If, for example, Michael indicates that, despite your "We are leaving now" announcement, he does not wish to go, and he must go because you have an appointment at home—well, then he will *go*. You pick him up, say, "Sorry, we're going," and cart him out the door. Even if he is screaming and carrying on. Admittedly, this is not the most pleasant way to accomplish things. If you are smart—and lucky—you can sometimes distract him, countering his "I don't wanna go!" with "Well, we must go. We're going to go home on the bus." The prospect of the bus ride (or whatever else Michael is known to favor) may be exciting enough to make him forget his desire to stay. It's also a nice gesture on your part—since he *is* trapped and must come and go at your whim.

Or take the dressing situation. If you have offered a choice of red overalls or blue overalls, and Michael responds with "I don't wanna put on *any* overalls," then—if it doesn't really make any difference to you, personally—you can simply say, "Okay, then you can stay in the house and *not* play in the sandbox." And that's that. Don't ever get into an argument with a small child unless (a) it's necessary and (b) you're prepared to win.

In issuing directives, it's important to take the child's level of understanding—and ability to concentrate—into account.

One child of three or four may be very well able to grasp and follow a series of instructions such as, "Go into your room, separate your toys from your sister's toys, pick yours up off the floor, and put them away neatly in the closet." Another child will simply be at sea; by the time you have gotten to the third step, he will have forgotten the first. It is often a good deal easier—on your nerves and on your throat—to go with him into the room, help him do the sorting, then go through the rest step by step: "Now, put these away. These blocks go on the shelf. Stack them neatly. This ball goes here, on the floor." Eventually he will get the idea. But be patient, and realistic in your demands.

Logic suggests, too, that you should in all fairness not expect your youngster to be a little automaton, responding instantly to your wishes. Children have thoughts and feelings too. If you have said to your child, "It will be bedtime soon, Rosemary, so put that pile of blocks away now," and you return to Rosemary's room ten minutes later to find her pulling her pajamas on, but the blocks are still in plain view, there may be a reason. And it may be perfectly valid. "That pile of blocks" in the middle of the floor may look haphazard to *you* —but to Rosemary it may be a castle or even an entire city. If you simply sweep them into the closet, you're destroying something that she has created. So you might ask, "Why didn't you put the blocks away?" If the reason does seem valid, bend a little bit: walk around the blocks, put Rosemary to bed, and let her continue her architectural project in the morning.

Strange People and/or Places

Sooner or later you will leave your youngster in the care of a grandparent, another relative, or a baby-sitter. The child will get used to this. But the first few times it's well to spell out your delegation of authority—i.e., make it perfectly clear that he is expected to behave in your absence just as though you were at home; although the orders will issue from someone else's mouth, he is to obey them, and no ifs, ands, or buts.

In general, outside your home, I don't think strangers have any business directing or disciplining your child—except, of course, to remove him from some clear and present danger. If some parent you encounter in the street or the park does not approve of your child's behavior, that's just too bad; your child is obliged only to follow your rules, not other people's ideas of what is right and proper and what is not.

When you are visiting someone else's home with the child, however, it *is* reasonable for your host or hostess to demand a certain amount of adherence to their house rules. You may not mind if your child draws pictures on the living-room wall, or jumps up and down on the couch, or races cars on the dining-room table—but other people may mind a great deal, and have every right to expect that their wishes will be respected. Children will accept distinctions—i.e., that certain things are acceptable under certain conditions and in certain places, but not permitted elsewhere—if you are specific.

Almost every family does permit some kinds of behavior that another family would consider reprehensible. Your youngster, I trust, is not being raised as a hermit; therefore you are doing him a great disservice if you do not draw these distinctions for him. And it will be your fault if, after a while, he is not welcome in other people's houses.

The same approach should be used when your child has begun to make friends with neighborhood youngsters, and—as in many communities—runs in and out of other children's homes. Michael should be told that when he is visiting Charlie Smith's house next door he is to follow whatever rules Mr. and Mrs. Smith have established for behavior in *their* home, even if they involve restrictions he is not required to observe in his own home.

There will be time enough, when your offspring are considerably older, for them to decide to flout society's rules of behavior and take the consequences. I do not think you should make that decision on their behalf.

Of Crimes and Punishments

It is important to realize that no punishment is effective unless the alternatives are understood clearly to start with. In other words, a choice must be presented: "Either you will do what I have asked you to do or you will be punished." And the consequences of the behavior in question must be understood as well.

You and I are well aware that if we toss a glass vase about on the patio it may fall on the flagstones and break; we know this because it's part of our past experience. But your three-year-old is not likely to really comprehend your warning, "Susie, don't play with that; it's breakable, and very valuable." Susie may actually be quite astonished when the vase falls from her fingers and shatters. Punishing her is not really appropriate. You simply have to explain that's what you meant, and clean it up, and say, "Next time, be careful."

When punishment *is* called for, the thing to do is administer it without delay. Small children have very short memories. "I'll tell your father when he comes home, and are you going to get it!"—when that event is six hours in the future—is ridiculous. By that time the child will have long since forgotten the exact nature of the transgression, and the punishment will be meaningless. Secondly, as they said in *The Mikado,* "let the punishment fit the crime"—at least as closely as possible.

Let us say that two-year-old Georgie is playing in the sandbox with a group of other children and he bites another child. This is a dangerous act and should be firmly discouraged.

You dash right over there, grab Georgie, and get his attention; you tell him that he is not ever to do that again, and that if he disobeys you he *will be punished*. You return to the bench, keeping a keen eye on Georgie. He does it again. Lose no time: immediately remove him from the sandbox and take him home. This is an appropriate deprivation, since he probably likes to play in the sandbox. (And if the act is repeated on another occasion, you might keep him out of the sandbox for several days.) Refusing to let him watch television, or play with his crayons, would not be punishments that fit the crime.

If, on the other hand, Georgie takes it into his head to scribble on the dining-room wall—again, if the subject has never come up before, you must make the alternatives clear. You might say, "You are not to do that again. You may draw on the special place on the wall in your own room, but you are not to use any other wall. If you do so again, your crayons will be taken away from you." Again, an appropriate punishment. And again, follow through if the act is repeated: take the crayons away, for at least a day or two—at which point Georgie will probably begin asking for them. He should be reminded, when the crayons are returned, of why they were taken away—and the specifics of where they may and may not be used should be repeated.

How about depriving a child of food? I don't think sending a child to bed without supper is ever a proper form of punishment. Nor do I think depriving a youngster of even a favorite food treat—e.g., ice cream for dessert—is appropriate, unless the crime itself is directly connected with food. (Desserts, in any case, should be nutritious and considered part of the meal.)

If he has deliberately, in defiance of your directives to use his spoon and eat neatly, dumped his spinach on the floor, a no-dessert punishment might be appropriate. Or if he has, earlier in the day, rammed an ice cream cone into his brother's face, you are justified in saying, "You obviously do not know how to handle ice cream properly, and you are not going to have ice cream for a few days." But I do not think it right to say, "Because you have not eaten your spinach you may not have your ice cream." Failure to ingest one food is no reason to be deprived of another.

It is, incidentally, possible in any of these situations that the error will never be repeated. Partly because the child wishes to avoid the announced punishment. But partly, too, in response to your initial displeasure. As I said earlier, children do, basically, want to win their parents' approval. Sometimes—not always, by a long shot—the disappointment or displeasure in your voice when you indicate what has been done wrong will be sufficient deterrent.

Do not, in any event, make idle threats. We have all witnessed scenes in which an exasperated mother says irately, "Johnny, if you don't stop that this very minute, we are going right home." Johnny, giving no sign that he has heard, keeps right on doing what he is doing, and his mother's next statement is, "Now come on, Johnny, stop doing that." Now he knows that she is not going to follow through. Or rather, he does not know *what* to believe. She may pick him up and take him home within the next thirty seconds. On the other hand, she may not. She has become completely unpredictable. And she has placed the child in a dilemma. Can he rely on any threats she makes? Can he rely on any promises whatever? Johnny is going to be pretty confused, since he is left without clear cause-and-effect premises on which to operate.

There are two forms of punishment I urge you not to use.

One is yelling. Very few parents can avoid yelling entirely, and that's understandable; there will be times when your patience is exhausted, and you will find yourself instinctively raising your voice. If these occasions are rare, the child will respond immediately, because the new and different tone of voice will startle him. But if you get into the habit of screaming at your child constantly, he will totally tune you out. Which will have two results, neither one desirable.

You will be hoarse by the end of the day. And because the child will learn to scream back at you, you will no longer converse in normal, conversational tones but will be trying to outshout each other continuously. This will leave you both exhausted. And child care will become a horrible burden, instead of the pleasure it should be.

Further, since your screaming has lost all special significance, some day when you shout at him as he is starting to cross the street in front of an oncoming car, he is not going to hear you.

Secondly, physical punishment. I think hitting a child is a very poor practice, chiefly because you are, by this action, suggesting a new form of behavior that does not occur instinctively in children. If you watch a group of small children playing together—children who have neither been hit themselves nor observed older youngsters fighting—you'll find that those who behave aggressively will push, pull, and occasionally bite; but they won't hit. If *you* hit the child, you are in fact demonstrating a form of behavior to him. And if you are doing it, it must be acceptable, right? You've told him, in other connections, that you want him to act "grown up," haven't you?

You have also introduced a distinct conflict by such action. Chances are you have taken some prior opportunity to point out that bullying, whether of younger siblings or smaller playmates, is not an acceptable form of behavior. Now here you are, hitting a three-year-old. And he looks up at you and says, "If I can't hit Jimmy, because he's littler than me—then how come you, a big person, can hit little me?" There is no answer, and there is egg all over your face. If he doesn't say it, he is thinking it. He is likely to reach the conclusion that bullying is okay after all, and may turn into the terror of the neighborhood. He will of course no longer trust any pronouncements of high principle on your part.

What if the child has taken it into his head to attack *you* physically? You must not permit it; we know that it can result in deep residual feelings of guilt in the child. But don't descend to his level and hit (or scratch or bite) him back. Simply seize the child's wrist(s) firmly. Say in firm, measured tones, "You are not to do that—ever." Hang onto him for at least a full minute. The child will inevitably realize that you possess vastly superior strength. When you let him go, he will feel bad, and there will be marks on his wrists—but you will not have done him any lasting damage, either physically or psychologically.

"What Do I Get if I'm Good?"

I won't keep you in suspense. I do *not* think children should be tangibly rewarded for behaving in the way they have been taught is correct. The best reward for a child is your pleasure, whether expressed or implied. And so far as ordinary day-to-day behavior is concerned, an absence of criticism is enough.

If, however, some out-of-the-ordinary event has occurred and you were particularly pleased by your youngster's behavior, by all means say so. If Johnny has for once appeared at the supper table with really clean hands and face, and you're pleased, there's nothing wrong with letting him know it: "Don't you look nice! You really did a good job!" If you are Johnny's mother, the comment, "Johnny was a good boy today," directed to Johnny's father, suggests that you didn't expect that to happen. But if you went out, it's perfectly appropriate to remark to Johnny's father, in Johnny's presence: "We went to visit Joey and Mrs. Smith this afternoon. Johnny and Joey played so nicely together. I was so proud of the way he behaved. And when Joey's baby sister fell down, he picked her up and made sure she didn't hurt herself."

In other words, giving Johnny or Susie a gold star at the end of the day simply for being "good" is silly. But if the only attention he or she gets from you is for *bad* behavior—well, you know what's going to happen. Thus it is very smart to dispense occasional praise for superb behavior, particularly if someone else, such as the other parent, is present to witness the kudos; that way, the child will tend to prefer the approved behavior. (Who wouldn't?) Don't compliment your youngster every time he or she puts the right foot in front of the left. But do single out special achievements—special to the *child*, not necessarily to *you*.

By the time your child is three or four you will find you can use him or her to help you with household tasks. This is not exploitation of child labor and it need not be paid for. Children, as it happens, love to help around the house. Work is an interesting activity, until someone tells them that it is a dirty word. They really enjoy it.

You can, by this age, ask Bobby to set the table, for instance. You will, of course, show him the proper way first. Then let him do it himself. Allow plenty of time before the meal. He will probably not do it right at first, and he will take a long time to do it wrong. But *don't do it over yourself*. If you do, he'll lose all incentive to do it right. Instead, show Bobby the proper way. And when he does produce the setting as you want it, compliment him—publicly, in front of the rest of the family. It will be a great source of pride.

Other tasks can be assigned—and similarly handled—based on your judgment of your youngster's abilities and expressed interests. Children are perfectly capable of sorting things (laundry, silverware, or anything else), drying silverware or other unbreakable things, assisting a parent by handing tools as they are needed, helping with such easy tasks as gardening ("Put each little plant in the hole, and then pat the dirt down"), placing pet food in a dish, performing simple cleaning jobs, helping with some kitchen chores, general fetching and carrying. They enjoy the privilege of participating in adult activities, and your praise for a job well done is payment enough.

A *Mantra* for *Tantra?*

If there were, in fact, a ritual incantation by which you would be assured that your child would never go into the performance we call a "temper tantrum," I would record it here. There unfortunately is not. So you had better be prepared.

Not that your youngster will necessarily get into this form of protest. Many children do not. But many do—and it is an indication of neither psychosis nor an incipient malevolence, merely a fairly low frustration tolerance. Typically, it involves an episode in which the child—usually one who is not terribly verbal—commences a performance involving assorted aural and visual components, including (variously) screaming, falling to the floor, kicking of heels, and/or banging of head and/or hands against the floor and/or walls (but he will not hurt himself, and don't let him convince you that he can). Temper tantrums generally do not occur after the child can express anger verbally, typically around the age of three.

If you have witnessed one such episode, I advise you to try to prevent recurrences. Avoid letting the child get overtired or hungry (hence, cranky). Try to intervene when you realize that the child's frustration tolerance is low; pleasant, relaxing activities such as warm baths can be helpful; so can light snacks such as cheese or fruit. You can also avoid triggering the response by particular things you know have provoked it before. These things may or may not work.

If Johnny does go into a tantrum, what to do depends in part on where you are. Generally, it is provoked by your refusal to grant some special request.

If you are at home, either ignore him completely or calmly pick him up and put him in his room. If you become visibly upset, or offer a reward for stopping the behavior, or give in to whatever the current demand may be, then he will have achieved his aim; and the performance will be repeated, because he knows it works. Repeat: the child is *not* psychotic; he is quite logical, and not stupid.

Once a child learns that this form of behavior does not shatter you, he will stop it. It is not really very enjoyable—and if it doesn't get results, it is not likely to be continued.

And if a temper tantrum takes place on the street or in a supermarket? The basic principles are no different. Your reaction, however, may well be—and understandably so. It is very embarrassing to be the object of curious stares as you drag a screaming, kicking youngster along the street or down the aisle of a supermarket. Try to keep your cool, difficult though it may be. You will feel that everyone is staring at you. They probably are. Some, because they have no other excitement in their lives; others, probably because they have been through precisely the same thing with their children and are aching to advise you.

Certainly if this has happened once I would suggest that you try to avoid any recurrence; it is pretty unsettling. The way to do so is to refrain from taking the child to public places for a while. Supermarkets happen to be a favorite location for public tantrums. If you cannot leave the child at home, shop early—when the child is least tired and cranky and the stores are least crowded. Early or late, keep your hands unencumbered, and see that the child is wearing soft shoes (if he's going to kick, make it as painless for yourself as possible). It is a good idea to invest in a small cart in which you can put your bundles; if both your arms are full of grocery bags, it's pretty hard to pick up a child.

This is an appropriate place to mention breath-holding, a special form of temper tantrum. It does not appear to be, at first glance, any such thing; it may seem that the child is losing either his mind or his life. It can be terrifying. Typically, the child who does this is a little more verbal than the ordinary temper-tantrum performer, since impact is important. He may well announce, "I am going to hold my breath until I turn blue!" Yes, he might do just that. He can lose consciousness or go into a convulsion. Do not panic, please; he *cannot kill himself.*

The moment a breath-holder starts to lose consciousness, the body's involuntary controls will automatically take over: the heightened carbon dioxide level in the child's blood will instantly trigger deep, rapid breathing, and the normal oxygen balance will be restored. But why let it get to this stage? If the child is sitting or standing on something soft, there will be no physical damage done; but if he isn't, he could, say, strike his head on something—and cause some real damage.

The question of potential danger aside, breath-holding is hardly a desirable habit, and it is wise to put a fast stop to the performance. You can do so by calmly and suddenly slapping the child's face. There will be an involuntary intake of breath, and that will be that.

How Active Is Hyperactive?

Sooner or later you are going to hear the term "hyperactive" (or "hyperkinetic," which means the same thing), if you have not heard it already. Perhaps you have read the word in newspapers or magazines. Or perhaps you know a child who is believed to be hyperactive. The word has been variously used, and sometimes misused, probably because its ordinary meaning and its medical meaning have been confused. Hyperactivity can be used, by anyone who wants to so use it, as a descriptive term—meaning, of course, simply *very active*. When it is used medically, and properly, it denotes something very specific; it is a neurological problem, and treatment may be indicated. I shall be using it, from here on, in the restricted, medical sense.

To the ordinary person, a "diagnosis" of hyperactivity in a toddler is often in the eye of the beholder, as it were. A very quiet, sedentary type of parent might consider a normally active, curious child terribly frenetic. Medically, hyperactivity is characterized not only by a great deal of random activity but also by a sort of intensity, a difficulty in adapting to new situations, and, prominently, an inability to concentrate on anything for more than a very brief period of time. If you are thinking that could describe most toddlers to some extent—you are absolutely right. That's why the diagnosis is so difficult in a preschooler. (It can even be difficult later, because of that subjective factor. In one recent study, nearly half of a group of young schoolboys were termed hyperactive—by their teachers. The actual incidence of true hyperactivity is perhaps 2 or 3 percent.)

If I am convinced that there is truly abnormal behavior of this kind in a patient, I refer the parent both to a pediatric neurologist and to a psychologist, so that the underlying cause can be determined. There may be an emotional problem, calling for therapy in that area. Should an organic difficulty be confirmed—i.e., if there is true hyperactivity—certain medications can be quite effective, in particular one called methylphenidate; amphetamines are also sometimes used, as is a more recently developed (and at this writing purely investigational) drug, pemoline. These are stimulant drugs, basically—that is, if given to an adult, or for that matter to a nonhyperactive child, they will have a pepping-up effect. In a truly hyperactive child, however, the result is quite the opposite: the youngster is calmed down, develops an ability to concentrate, and on the whole functions much more effectively. Though these are psychoactive drugs, there is no danger if they are properly used; they are not continued indefinitely, and no habituation or dependence is created.

Should you suspect your youngster may be hyperactive, the question should be discussed with your doctor. The child may need treatment of one sort or another. But the odds are against it.

Parents must realize that by the time a child is two or three years old he has a personality of his own—which may be totally different from his mother's or father's. Sometimes a parent's demands will simply be too restrictive for the child who is naturally curious and energetic. Confine a very physical child, who needs to run and jump, in a small city apartment, and you are going to have a very restless creature who seems never to sit still for a moment. Put that same child in a rural context, where he has room to move around and is not enclosed by four walls, and he will appear to be—and will be—a perfectly normal preschooler.

Frequently, when a parent complains to me that a three- or four-year-old is "impossibly" frenetic and "must be hyperactive," I know perfectly well what the problem is, because I know the parent and I know the child. I simply take out my prescription pad and write: A TRIP TO THE PARK. TAKE TWICE A DAY.

8

Kissing Kin: Smart Solutions for Sibling Problems

Before there are sibling problems, there must be siblings. I hate to lead off with such an obvious statement, but there it is. No problems can arise between your first-born and his or her brother(s) and/or sister(s) if there are none of the latter. Thus, if you would avoid all possibility of "sibling problems" —a term I have used for want of a better one, and because it's commonly understood—then, clearly, do not provide your child with any siblings.

I hasten to add that I am not advocating that course of action. I can recall practically no only child I have met, male or female, old or young, who has expressed a desire to limit his or her own family to only one child. It is my feeling that there is probably some distinct lack a single child feels (something I cannot personally verify, since I am not an only child).

The decision regarding the number of children you will have, which may of course range upward from zero, is in my view entirely up to you. Some couples I have known are talented enough, and patient enough, to raise an infinite number of children (if you are thinking that such parents should increase the size of their families by adopting otherwise unwanted youngsters, I would perhaps agree). Others, because of their own predilections, would probably do well—for themselves as well as their small charges—to remain childless.

If you are reading this chapter in a state of indecision about having a second or subsequent child—whether naturally or by adoption—I cannot tell you what decision to make. That conclusion must be reached by you and your spouse alone, based upon your own circumstances and beliefs. I *would* postulate two possibly helpful guidelines:

1. Don't have a second child "for the sake of" the first. A child is not a toy. You are not going to discharge your responsibility to provide the first with human companionship by acquiring a contemporary for him.

2. Don't feel that you are doing the first child some sort of injustice if you feel you would like to produce, or adopt, another. While enriching the life of the first is not a reason for having a second child, it tends to be a result. If you enjoy having children, that is a perfectly fine emotion; there is no reason for you to feel guilty about "foisting" the newcomer on the first child.

There is no generally agreed-upon "ideal" interval between siblings; again, it's a matter of the parents' personal points of view. Many psychologists—though by no means all—suggest three years, for purely practical reasons: by the time the second child is born, the first has generally progressed pretty well along the path to feeding himself and taking himself to the toilet. Even greater spacing has advantages, too. A six-year-old, for example, can be of real assistance in caring for an infant—and the two will be in college at different times, probably getting married at different times, etc., thus spreading the financial burden a bit thinner.

Some parents prefer, on the other hand, to deliberately "group" their offspring—going through the baby-care stage just once (though for a longer time) rather than repeatedly; one adoptive couple I know now has children aged two and a half years, eighteen months, and six months, and plans to adopt a fourth when child number three reaches the age of one year. It's true, too, that youngsters close in age are far more likely to become, and remain, good friends.

Fair Warning

There is no reason for you to go into a frenzy concerning potential feelings of insecurity on the part of a youngster when a sibling's arrival is imminent. On the other hand, it is not quite fair to spring this sort of thing at the last minute; the presence of another person in the house—on a permanent basis—takes a bit of getting used to, and it is nice to let the older child prepare himself for the event.

When and how you inform young Michael that Johnny or Jeannie is on the way depends in good part on the child's age and understanding, as well as on his own curiosity. I do feel that he should hear the news no later than you inform your friends and/or relatives. Certainly at least a month's warning is called for; if Michael hasn't queried *you* by this time, and he is old enough to understand English, it is time you offered some information. If he does initiate the subject himself, it will be because he has observed something out of the ordinary, and his question is likely to be along the lines of "Hey, Daddy, how come Mommy is getting so fat?" Or "Who's going to sleep in that baby bed?"

What you say must be played by ear. Obviously, if the child asks a direct question, the place to begin is with the answer to that question: "Mommy looks that way right now because there is a new baby growing inside her," or "This bed is going to be for your new baby brother or sister." If a specific question is not asked, just start with a simple announcement of the fact and then see what the child does ask or what comment he makes. Don't fear that you will have to give an illustrated lecture on the human reproductive system; a small child's curiosity stops far short of that.

He may or may not be interested in how the baby got where it is. He will probably wonder just *where* the baby is, however. Don't say it's in his mother's stomach; he has a stomach too, remember. Advising him that "mommies have a special place inside for babies to grow until they are big enough to be born" will take care of it—and if he wants to know what it's called, by all means tell him it's a uterus. How will the baby emerge? "The doctor will help the baby be born." That's about it, unless he asks further questions (see Chapter 12). What Michael will be concerned with, having absorbed the fact of the baby's imminent arrival, is what Johnny's or Jeannie's presence will mean to *him*. Basically, although he cannot verbalize it, he will be fearful that the new arrival will supplant him in some way in your eyes.

It is good to do everything you can to reassure the older child—though you cannot offer complete reassurance, and I don't advise you to try. The baby *will* take up a good deal of your time and effort, and there is no way of getting around that fact. The older child *will* feel some jealousy, and there is no getting around that fact either.

So long as the problem is a future one, there is not going to be any difficulty; small children have very hazy concepts of time, and "a few weeks," or "two months," is not a particularly meaningful phrase. When the mother dashes off to the hospital, however, it will be clear that events have taken a specific turn, and something is surely about to happen. At this point, it is helpful to put yourself in the child's place. His mother has gone off, Lord knows where, to acquire another child. His father, too, seems rather absorbed in this event. Suddenly—and it will seem sudden, no matter what careful explanations you have offered ahead of time—he is not the center of attention. There is a New Baby on the horizon.

One small but valuable step is to remain in touch. The mother—who has usually been around every day—will be spending several days in the hospital. Some hospitals permit small children to visit; others do not. Visiting will help. If it is not allowed, a phone call—directly to the child—at least once a day will tell him in no uncertain terms that, wherever Mommy is, she is obviously thinking about him. She might, too, relate whatever she has to say about the new baby to the older sibling (keyed, of course, to the circumstances): "The new baby is a boy, and what do you think of the name Johnny for him?" Or, "Jeannie has blue eyes, just like yours." Above all: "I have really missed you."

A word, speaking of names, about names. In general, I think it is good to make them as distinct as possible, so that each child enjoys his or her own identity with no confusion or question. It is well for parents to look ahead a little. There are three situations I have seen which can lead to later mix-ups, hence are best avoided. One is identical initials; if a letter is addressed, or a school notebook is marked, simply, "J. A. Brown," and the Brown children are named John Andrew, Jane Ann, and Jeremy Arthur, there could be difficulties. A second: names that sound similar, e.g., Johnny and Bonnie, Kathy and Jackie, Morris and Doris. And, third, names with a potential for being abbreviated to the same, or sound-alike, nicknames—Christopher and Christine, Patricia and Patrick, Joseph and Josephine (or Joan), John (which often becomes Jack) and Jacqueline, Edward (or Edmond) and Bette (or Elizabeth), Caroline and Lawrence (Larry), Martin and Martha, etc.

And Now—He-e-ere's Johnny!

There is, as I have said, going to be a certain amount of hostility, no matter what anyone says, when the new baby has been brought home from the hospital. It is a very good idea to bring the older child a doll—of the same sex as the baby—when you bring the baby home. Any aggressive feelings can be vented harmlessly upon the doll. This is normal.

Do not conclude, if Michael dismembers his boy doll, that he is some sort of incipient sadist and that little Johnny's life is in imminent danger.

On the other hand, don't leave the children alone together either—even for a split second—at this early stage. Hostile feelings aside, a preschooler simply does not know how to deal with an infant safely. Even if no malice is felt or intended, there will be a great deal of curiosity. (It looks like a child, but just lies there, and it often has a peculiar lack of hair and other accouterments.) Small fingers can get poked into even smaller eyes. There is no understanding of the fragility of a newborn baby; the older child is likely to handle the infant as roughly as he does his toys—and the infant is completely defenseless against that onslaught. It's fine for the older child to hold and play with the younger—but only under your watchful eye.

This will not go on forever; eventually, it will be perfectly safe to leave the children alone together. You will know when that time has arrived; every parent does. In the meantime, if you do not want to assume twenty-four-hour guard duty, it is well to keep the door to the newborn baby's room closed and secured in a way the older youngster can't undo—such as a hook-and-eye closure that the shorter parent has to stretch to reach.

Although you must protect the new baby from physical attack (and the older child from deep and damaging guilts that often follow such attack) it's also important to recognize the older child's feelings and permit him to express them in words. There is no way you can rationalize these feelings away. Nor will punishing the elder for expressing them do any good. I assure you it will not make any sense to three-year-old Michael if you say, "Michael, how on earth can you possibly say you hate your brother Johnny? That is sinful, and nasty, and I do not ever want to hear you say anything like that again." If you say that to him, he may avoid making such remarks in your presence. But his feelings will remain unchanged.

This may be difficult for you to understand. It is helpful to try to look at the situation from a child's standpoint. *You* may find the new baby lovable and fascinating. But, to a three-year-old, what good is a child who doesn't talk, doesn't run around and play, just lies there taking food in at one end, soiling the other end, and taking up parental time and effort previously devoted to him? The closest analogy I can think of: how would you feel if your spouse brought home another wife (or husband)—assuming this were legally permissible—and announced that, though his/her love for you had not lessened a whit, he/she now had room in his/her heart for another? Even if you eventually accepted the setup and the interloper ultimately became your best friend, wouldn't your nose be considerably out of joint for a while?

Let Michael know that you understand and appreciate his feelings about little Johnny, even if you don't share and approve of them, and that you are confident he will cope with the situation satisfactorily after a while. The baby is certainly not going to be returned from whence he came (a solution that is sometimes brightly offered by the older child).

Essentially, your challenge is to balance your time, insofar as you can, so that each child's needs are served. It really *isn't* right to devote so much time to the younger child that there is none left for the elder, or to force the elder to share *his relationship with you* (what you're trying to convince him of, remember, is that you are perfectly capable of loving, caring for, and being interested in him—despite the new baby's presence and legitimate claims upon you). I think it is a good idea for each parent to try to spend some part of each day alone with each child, both now and as they grow older—time during which interruptions (coping with minor household crises, answering telephone calls, accepting drop-in visits from neighbors) are discouraged.

I said each child—not just the elder. Don't fall into the trap of feeling so sorry for him that you neglect the younger. The baby is, after all, a permanent addition to the family. If you seem to ignore him when he is apparently upset, uncomfortable, lonely, or whatever, the older child might well conclude that sometime he might be in the same boat. This can make him very uneasy. If he insists upon your attention while you are occupied with the baby, make it perfectly clear that you are caring for the infant precisely as you did for him when he was that age, you intend to finish what you are doing, and you will *then* turn your attention to him.

There is one other question that may come up during these very early months. That concerns your feeding of the baby. Whether the route is breast or bottle, the older child may well query you about it if he is no longer fed by that method. Small children, in general, do not make a psychological distinction between breast and bottle; the question, if it is asked, is mainly an expression of curiosity and does not have adult connotations. It generally comes in the form of, "How come Johnny drinks his milk that way, and I drink mine from a bottle (or cup)?" The best answer, as in most such situations, is the truth, simply phrased: "All babies are fed that way, and so were you when you were a baby. Now that you're a big boy (or girl), you drink your milk the way big boys (or girls) do." Occasionally, the youngster who has been off the bottle for quite some time will issue a disconcerting demand: he will want to *try* the breast or bottle. Let him. He won't enjoy it or find it comfortable, and he won't ask again.

Love, It's Wonderful (Is That the Kid He Used to Despise?)

At some point you will be astonished to find the older child actually begins to like the younger. Not surprisingly, this generally happens when the baby develops some faculty of communication—when he starts to smile, coo, and gurgle, generally at two, three, or four months. This makes him a lot more interesting. Often, too, the baby will bestow his biggest smiles and expressions of pleasure upon his older sibling. This makes him even more interesting; it is pretty hard to continue to resent a small creature who obviously delights in you and breaks into a grin whenever you appear.

Since the baby responds so nicely, the older child will now start to regard him as at least a potential playmate. It's still not a good idea to leave them alone together just yet. But certainly encourage interaction in your presence—and if the older child's caresses seem a bit rough to you, don't worry or interfere, so long as the baby isn't crying and is not being hurt. Remember he's now bigger and older and not as fragile as he used to be.

You may find, as this relationship blossoms, that—despite the fact that the baby cannot yet talk—some mysterious form of direct communication arises between the two children. I cannot tell you how or why this occurs, and perhaps the explanation in *Mary Poppins*—that it is a faculty we simply lose as we grow older—is as good as any. It can be, in any event, very handy. If it happens, don't question it; just consider yourself lucky, because the older child—if he has learned to communicate in the conventional manner with you—can perform useful service as an interpreter. Often, when you are at your wit's end trying to figure out just why the baby is crying, and if he wants a bottle, whether he would rather have milk, water, or juice—the older child will matter-of-factly inform you that the baby is "saying" that he would like some orange juice. In a significant percentage of instances, the translation will turn out to be absolutely correct.

Soon it will be safe to leave the children alone together. As I said earlier, you will know when this stage has arrived. You may decide, then, that you want them to share a room. I have no hard-and-fast advice on this subject; the decision is the family's and depends upon a number of variables—

primarily, of course, the size of your living quarters, but also on the personalities and sleep needs of the children. I have not seen any consistent psychological effects stemming either from having a room of one's own or from sharing with a sibling.

If you do want the children to share, it is a good idea to discuss it first with the elder; he will be flattered by being given some say in the decision. If he says absolutely not, he does not want the baby to sleep in the same room, wait awhile; his adamant attitude means the arrangement would not yet be safe for the baby. Most older children are—or will shortly be—delighted to be entrusted with the responsibility, and they like having the company, too. Often, in fact, if the youngsters in question are of the same sex, and each has his very own room, they will *ask* to share—using one of the two rooms as a shared bedroom, the other as a shared playroom. I do feel it is a good idea, when children share a room, to divide the room in some way—not necessarily with a floor-to-ceiling barrier, but with some demarcation of their respective territories, each containing that child's own toys, books, clothing, etc.

Typically, during this period when the earlier sibling's attitude changes, there is an interesting behavior reversal. Now, if you can manage to sneak up on the two of them, you may be pleasantly astounded to find just how gently the elder treats the younger. In your presence, though, the elder may deliberately taunt or manhandle the baby—not with intent to hurt, but because he knows that it's a very good way to get your attention. (Watch out. This is the first indication that they may be in league against you.)

Judge and Jury

You will find, as the children grow older, that you will be cast in the role of omnipotent arbitrator. There are going to be crises. They may be friends, but they are going to have disagreements. I have talked about general behavior problems in an earlier chapter—but there are some that are peculiar to siblings, because there is a built-in, ever present rivalry. The disagreements will tend to fall, very generally, into two categories.

One: the squabbles that inevitably arise between the children, having nothing to do with your relationship to either one. Typically, you will be calmly preparing dinner, reading a book, or talking on the telephone, when you hear sounds of apparent warfare from the back yard, the playroom, or wherever the children have supposedly been engaging in a quiet, cooperative game of one sort or another.

This advice may be difficult to follow, but the smart move is to *leave them alone*—unless the sounds emanating from the play area (a) are bloodcurdling screams or (b) vastly exceed your personal level of noise tolerance. In the first instance, you will want to rescue whichever child is being, presumably, tortured or maimed. In the second, you will want to—and have every right to—demand that you and other members of the family be permitted the peace and quiet you deserve.

If one of these factors has led you to investigate, your first aim, of course, will be to find out if one of the children has in fact been injured—whether by the other or via some accident. In a percentage of cases I would not care to specify, although my feeling is that it is in the upper nineties, you will not find an emergency case. What you are likely to encounter is something resembling nothing so much as a courtroom in which—without specific charges or even a single word from you—the advocates have both commenced simultaneous (and often deafening) pleas of self-defense. These are usually along the lines of, "He hit me first!" or "She knocked over my blocks!" or sometimes simply, "It wasn't *me!*" Typically, both participants will glare at you, cast sidelong glances at the other, and hope that they have successfully warded off any accusation of being the initiator of the trouble.

I urge you to refuse to listen to any of the detailed briefs. Because if you do, and you start trying to play Justice Balancing the Scales, you are going to get into deep trouble. And you will not get anything else done for the rest of the day. Simply say something along the lines of, "Well, as long as you cannot play together nicely and quietly, I am going to have to separate you. When you are ready to behave in a friendly manner, you may then play together again." And at this point you dispatch one child to one room or area and the other to some separate place. It is an entirely appropriate punishment, and the worst that can be meted out under the circumstances.

And it works. By not playing referee, you save a great deal of time and energy. That is always a good thing. You will also find that after you have used this method two or three times the difficulty will crop up less and less often: the children will learn from experience; they are not going to repeatedly ply you with conflicting stories if they know in advance that you are not going to pay any attention to them. One day you may be startled to hear a swiftly suppressed scream from the next room followed by a loudly whispered admonition: "Ssshh! If you make too much noise, Mommy'll come in and make one of us go upstairs!"

I would add one other piece of advice pertaining to such a situation. Don't assign burdensome responsibilities to one sibling just because he or she happens to be the elder. A four-year-old is a four-year-old and is not ready to assume the role of responsible nursemaid simply because the other party to the controversy happens to be two and a half. Thus a statement such as, "You're older, so you should know better than to . . ." is foolish, does not work, and serves only to foster antagonism in the child you have singled out; that antagonism, I might add, is likely to persist long past childhood. At the same time, such an approach can well encourage the younger to *avoid* all responsibility for his or her actions—an attitude that can give rise to all sorts of troublesome situations later in life.

The second sort of situation in which you will be asked to play judge and jury involves you directly; it is a competition for your favor and, simultaneously (because your favor, for your child, is a clue to his or her own self-esteem), a running self-versus-sibling comparison. Don't encourage it.

Each will want to be "first." This will take the form of such statements as, "You held her hand yesterday, so you have to hold my hand today." Or, "Last time, he got the biggest apple, so this time I get the biggest apple." Once you start playing this game, you can't stop—since, by going along with it, you've implicitly accepted the rules, and woe betide you if you get caught in an infraction. It is far safer to reject the premise in the first place. Love is not measured by the size of an apple, and it is well to make this very clear to your children. If you let your children vie for your favor on such flimsy premises, they are going to get some very odd ideas about how one achieves success in life.

A corollary to this rule is one regarding birthdays. Perhaps, in your family, you pay little or no attention to birthdays, and that may be the smartest move (one family I know has a cardinal rule: nothing more elaborate than a card for anyone's birthday; gifts are reserved for Christmas). But if you do recognize birthdays in your family, don't feel that you must get Susie a gift because you are buying a birthday present for Jimmy. Susie will presumably get a gift on her own birthday. (If, on the other hand, you are in a store with one child and it is not a special occasion but you consent to purchase a toy for that child, it is good to encourage some thinking about the child who is not on the shopping trip. Actually, this is sometimes not necessary; the child may think of it himself, and spontaneously remark, "Can we bring something home for Susie?")

Birthdays can also lead to other difficulties. They generally arise when a parent has made an arbitrary statement such as, "Barbara is five, and therefore she can stay up until eight o'clock. When you are five, you may stay up until eight. Until then, you will go to bed at seven."

In fact, as I have noted in Chapter 4, sleep needs are not necessarily dependent on birthdays; a child of four may conceivably need more sleep than a child of two. You are doing the child a distinct disservice if you arbitrarily change his or her bedtime on a particular date, birthday or other.

By the same token, you are drawing artificial lines if you peg any other privileges—or responsibilities—to birthdays. Neither should be age-dependent but should relate to the individual. And you may find, by the way, that a younger sibling is ready to assume some responsibilities earlier than the older one did—simply because he or she can learn from the older child.

Two at a Time

Twins may or may not present special problems for the parents (aside from the obvious nuisance of having double the number of dirty diapers, two children going through the same learning stages at the same time, etc.). It depends upon what kind of twins they are.

Twins of opposite sexes are of course simply a brother and sister who happen to have been born at the same time. There is not going to be any confusion as to who is who, and the situation is essentially no different from that of any siblings who are close in age.

Fraternal twins of the same sex are also simply two brothers, or two sisters, born at the same time, and are just as different—in talents, abilities, interests—as any other two brothers or sisters. Except that they *are* the same age, which can lead to some early confusion if they resemble each other fairly closely. By the time they are of school age, fraternal twins generally look quite distinct. But prior to that time strangers (not the parents or other family members or close friends) may have trouble telling them apart, since they may well have the same color hair and eyes and be identical or nearly identical in size (later, of course, they will not; I have never known a family in which all the offspring grew to precisely the same adult height). It is good to prevent such confusion and foster individuality from the start by giving them dissimilar names, dressing them differently, and encouraging any other distinctions (such as tastes in clothing, hair length, and the like) that develop along the way.

Identical twins, of course, present a real problem. Or perhaps I should call it a challenge. Since they share a common genetic make-up, they will not only look alike, but in their early years will tend to think and behave similarly as well (later life experiences of each will play a part in developing their distinct personalities). Sometimes even the parents cannot always tell them apart; certainly others will have difficulty. I think it is quite important to establish individual identities; as with fraternal twins of the same sex, it is advisable to dress them differently, give them names that are not susceptible to confusion, etc. To make things easier for others, especially when they first encounter large groups of strangers (when they start attending nursery school or kindergarten, for instance), you might embroider some of their clothes with names or initials.

Identical twins are usually very close. By the time they are walking and talking, they are typically fast friends and have a deeper understanding of, and sympathy with, each other than other siblings—hence will probably squabble a good deal less.

They will also find it great fun to fool others, as soon as they discover that people cannot tell them apart. You cannot interfere with this closeness, nor should you try. But I do think it is a good idea, since they will choose to spend so much time together, to make sure that they spend some time apart, as well. If circumstances permit, try to enroll them in separate kindergartens, play groups, etc., where they can make their own friends, and where each can be judged on his or her own, without comparison with the other.

Will the "Real" Brother Please Stand Up?

Increasingly, parents of one or more natural children are choosing to increase the size of their families by adoption. This need not present any special problem; natural and adoptive children will accept one another readily if the situation is well presented to them.

This means that a balance must be struck. If you have adopted five children and have no others, you can praise to the skies the merits and superiority of deliberate choice ("We picked you out personally; unlike some other children, you were really wanted . . ."). But if you have some of each, you obviously must not oversell that way of acquiring offspring, since your natural children will begin to feel thrust upon you by mere happenstance—i.e., not chosen, and possibly not wanted.

I think if you are careful to emphasize that all your children are definitely wanted and loved—equally—there will be no real problem, and the children will feel quite secure and equally close to you and to one another. Sibling love stems from being raised together, being loved and cared for by the same parents, rather than from sharing the same biological heritage. In families I have known, natural and adopted children have grown up just as close, sharing just as strong family bonds, as siblings with the same natural parents.

9

Playthings, Animate and Otherwise

You may contemplate acquiring a pet for your youngster—
or the pet may in fact precede the child as a member of your
family. You will certainly entertain the idea of providing
your tot with toys. In this chapter I shall offer some of my
own thoughts on these subjects, plus some purely factual admonitions that are important for the sake of your youngster's
health and safety, as well as your own peace of mind.

Pets, Prospects and Aspects

If you already own a dog or cat when your first child
is born, be prepared for a brief period of jealousy on the animal's—particularly a dog's—part. This is a perfectly natural
response, since the pup has in most ways been treated like a
baby (fed, led somewhere for elimination, played with,
petted, talked to) and has previously enjoyed your exclusive
attention. After a while your pet will—like a sibling—accept
the baby, and will in fact become quite protective. Despite
stories and rumors you may have heard, I have not known of
an adult dog or cat injuring or harming a newborn baby. You

will, of course, want to introduce your pet to the infant; when you are satisfied that the animal has no malicious intent, it is perfectly safe to leave the pet in the room with the baby.

But if you are like many of the first-time parents I've known, you'll think about getting a pet *after* the child has come along.

For a number of reasons, I think a dog is probably the best sort of pet for a very small child—although I would not exclude a kitten from consideration. Dogs, as a rule, respond most affectionately and gently to small humans; cats tend, though there are certainly exceptions, to go their own way a good deal, thus may not make great playmates.

In any case, I do think it important to get either a young animal or one that has been raised with children (but be sure it has never been mistreated by a child). An animal unused to the quick and unpredictable movements of youngsters (or one that has previously been ill-treated by a child) is likely to become frightened at such movements and to feel that they are a threat. A threatened animal may make some sudden movements of its own, with disastrous results for the child. An animal raised from puppyhood or kittenhood in a home with active children will accept their roughhousing and running about as a natural state of affairs.

I would not, by the way, advise your acquiring a few-weeks-old puppy when you have a few-weeks-old baby, simply because new puppies need almost as much care and attention as new babies: they must be fed several times a day, they have to be toilet-trained, they need to be taken to the doctor for shots, they go through teething, they have to be supplied with toys, etc. One new baby is enough to cope with at one time, unless you have boundless energy.

How you go about getting a pet is up to you. But whether you acquire it by gift, purchase, a visit to the pound, or it arrives on your doorstep one day and just sits there demanding to be adopted—*have it checked out thoroughly by a veterinarian and given a clean bill of health*, before you bring it into your home. This holds true especially for strays; you do not know how far and how long it has strayed, and animals can pick up many undesirable things, externally and internally, in their wanderings.

What about other kinds of pets? Certain kinds should wait, I think, until a child is at least six years old, and perhaps considerably older. That statement includes snakes, gerbils, guinea pigs, hamsters, goldfish, etc. Adult members of the family are unlikely to find such animals very interesting companions. They are generally purchased expressly for the child, who assumes care of the pet—and I don't think even a five-year-old is capable of doing so. (If an older child in your family does have a gerbil, guinea pig, hamster, or the like, let me answer here a question I am often asked. Though these animals do nip little fingers frequently, they are laboratory-raised, and your youngster cannot get rabies from such a bite.)

Birds? Fine for watching and listening to—but see that the child has no direct access to the bird, for the sake of both. Birds are too fragile to be handled by young children. And an annoyed bird's beak can inflict serious injury. Also, if you have any history of allergy in your family, it is better not to bring a bird into the home; allergy to dander from feathers (which is dispelled constantly into the air) is very common, and the resultant reactions—not excluding severe asthma—can be extremely unpleasant.

If you have been thinking about a pet turtle for your three-year-old, think again. A 1971 study revealed that pet turtles are frequently sources of salmonella infections, and such infections can be critical matters. (The turtles involved have become contaminated with the bacteria on the southern

farms where they were bred, not at neighborhood pet shops.)
A full third of the cases researched were severe enough to require ten days of hospitalization—and most of the victims
were children under the age of five years. It is estimated that
pet turtles may have been causing up to 20 percent of all salmonella infections recorded in the U.S.—perhaps as many as
40,000 each year.

I should add that, as this is written, the Public Health
Service has announced protective regulations banning impor-
tation of pet turtles and requiring disease-free certification
for such turtles prior to interstate shipment. If such regulations are in fact effective, and achieve their intended goal, by
the time you read this, I can see no other objection to purchasing a turtle for your youngster. They're fun and easy to
care for, and it's well-nigh impossible for either child or turtle
to injure the other.

I probably need not add—but I will anyway, for the sake of
completeness—that creatures whose natural habitat is the
jungle, the outback, or the Serengeti, including monkeys,
lion cubs, and the like, belong there or in a zoo, and not in
your home.

Some comment on safety matters is appropriate. HEW
estimates the number of annual injuries perpetrated by pets
at some 350,000, and many unofficial estimates range up to
twice that many. Most of the injuries involve dogs, and most
of the victims are children. This does not mean that dogs are
by nature vicious; 99 percent of them are not. It does mean
that they—and cats too—are *capable* of injury. A vast majority of such injuries are preventable.

Certainly the basic rule, which you should impress upon
your child, is that a pet must be recognized as a personality
to be respected; the average child under two or three years is
not capable of grasping this notion—hence should never be
left alone with a dog or cat. A pet is to be cherished and

played with—not teased, taunted, or otherwise molested; a threatened animal (or one that believes it is threatened), as I noted earlier, will naturally and normally strike out in self-defense. A number of investigators feel that up to 90 percent of all dog bites involve pets or other dogs known to the victims—and that in most cases the victim is a child who has teased or mistreated the animal. Even a toddler who doesn't intend to be mean can inadvertently hurt or frighten an animal.

Do permit child and pet to play together *in your presence.* You'll find that cats and dogs, particularly the latter, are generally very friendly and protective toward young humans, just as they are toward their own young. Don't worry if your puppy, for example, licks your baby; it is an expression of affection, and there is no recorded case of friendly licking doing an infant any harm.

Generally speaking, tame animals will not stage unprovoked attacks upon humans. This is particularly true of dogs and cats; they have been bred as pets for generations, and most of them feel a definite affection toward their owners—and, by extension, toward others to whom the owners behave in a friendly manner. If an animal you own attacks even one person for absolutely no reason—and you are *sure* there was not the slightest provocation—that animal is not behaving normally, and you should get rid of it.

Of course you should keep your pet in good health and see that it receives rabies shots and any others your vet recommends. Be aware, too, that animals can act as inadvertent carriers of troublemaking substances. Oils from poison-ivy plants, for instance; dogs aren't allergic to them, but most humans are. Ticks and fleas hitching a ride on your dog's coat can carry a number of infections—again, not to the dog but to your youngster. Both small children *and* small dogs are susceptible to ringworm—which has sometimes been picked up from unsanitary clippers in grooming establishments (both human and animal).

One special word about cats, applying only if you are *expecting* a child. There is a widespread, and typically mild, parasitic infection called toxoplasmosis, a fairly minor kind of respiratory infection—in fact so minor that the person who has it may not even feel especially ill. But toxoplasmosis in a pregnant woman can sometimes cause damage to an unborn baby, damage similar to that resulting from rubella. Two sources of infection have been pinpointed. One is raw or undercooked meat; the other is cat feces.

Cats are not susceptible to the illness themselves, but if they become infected, they do serve as the vehicle for a particular stage of the parasite's life cycle. A cat becomes infected by something *it* has eaten—a bird or rodent, for instance. If you are a mother-to-be and you own a cat, it would be wise to find out if you are susceptible to toxoplasmosis; a simple blood test can tell you. So far as is known, having had the illness makes one immune—and remember that you may have had it without its being diagnosed or even noticed.

If you find you are susceptible, the National Foundation-March of Dimes, which concerns itself with birth defects and their prevention, suggests four protective steps:

1. Have your cat's kitty litter changed daily—by someone else, not you; the person who does it should wear rubber gloves.

2. Feed your cat only commercial cat food, whether dry or canned; don't let it go out on hunting expeditions.

3. Don't do any gardening during your pregnancy if there's any possibility that your cat—or any other cat—might have defecated in the vicinity; when feces work their way into the soil, the infective organisms can remain active for months.

4. Don't pet or play with other people's cats during your

pregnancy—and if you're thinking of getting a new cat, put it off till after the baby arrives.

Babes and Toyland

One shrewd couple I know has developed a practice that might well be pursued by other annually distraught parents. Each Christmas season their young children are taken on a conducted tour of a certain large and prominent Fifth Avenue toy emporium. They are encouraged to look and marvel at the vast array of gadgetry, to examine to their heart's delight each doll, each hand-painted rocking horse, each painstakingly crafted miniature car and truck. And they are told that, unfortunately, this place is a museum and that not a single one of these wondrous items is for sale.

I don't know, actually, if they really tell their youngsters that; the story may be purely apocryphal. But it does illustrate the extent to which the American parent is pressed to part with huge wads of cash—not just at Christmas, though the promotional barrage is particularly heavy and insistent then, but all year round. A few figures bear out the impression. There are approximately 1,200 toy manufacturers in the U.S.; they produce an estimated $2,500,000,000 to $3,000,000,000 worth of toys every single year. In addition, some 83,000 shipments of toys from foreign sources annually enter our country.

It is no wonder that the average parent is both bewildered about how to choose toys for his or her child and outraged by the deep dent the toy industry manages to make in the family budget. Let me add another reason for indignation: every year, by U. S. Public Health Service estimates, there are no less than 700,000 injuries associated with toys. I have before me the list of toys banned—because they were judged hazardous—by the Food and Drug Administration's Bureau of

Product Safety over one five-month period, December 1971 through April 1972; they total no less than 129 items (each, of course, distributed by the thousands). Nor are the sources of such toys necessarily Unknown & Anonymous, Ltd., of Hong Kong. There are quite a few extremely prominent names—of exclusive shops and nationwide chains, of respected mail-order firms, even of makers of so-called "educational" toys—on the list. These 129 toys were, of course, only those that the BPS's small surveillance staff happened to lay hands on.

I'll come back to the hazard problem and how to avoid it. First, let's start with a rather basic and relevant question: does a child really *need* any toys?

Children do need to play; of that there is no doubt whatever. There is a great deal of doubt as to whether a newborn baby needs a contraption that was introduced in late 1971 (I quote from a magazine article describing it): a "three-level baby crib equipped with toys to grasp and pull, sand timers to watch, wheels to spin, voice-activated mobiles with sound tapes, plus a tank awash with live fish." No, I am not joking. And an infant cannot even focus his eyes properly on a *stationary* object until he is at least eight or nine weeks old. Funny? The designer was probably convulsed with laughter all the way to the bank, as they say.

In fact a child under the age of one year does not need *any* toys, per se. Why? Because everything is essentially a toy, including his own body. Define a toy as a new sensation, a new something to see, or hear, or touch, and perhaps do something with—and watch your six-week-old offspring having a ball with his fingers and toes—and you'll see what I mean. You'll also understand why a toddler doesn't differentiate between "his" toys and adult objects meant for other functions.

Sure, get the youngster a mobile for his crib, if you like—

one mobile, not a three-ring circus—and maybe a very simple "busy box" for his playpen, when he's old enough to sit in a playpen. As he starts to crawl, and maybe toddle about a bit, you can add adventure in the form of—just for starters— wooden spoons, saucepans, clothespins (the classic kind, not the pinch type), wooden bowls (e.g., salad bowls), outsize wooden spools that can roll across the floor, smaller spools strung on a sturdy cord, egg cartons, chunks of tissue paper, scrap paper and nontoxic crayons, empty boxes and cartons (crawling holes can be cut in the latter), unbreakable table- ware, smoothly sanded and brightly painted wooden blocks (any shape, not necessarily uniform; only factories have to turn out uniform products). None of which *you* find espe- cially intriguing, but all of which will—believe me—be fasci- nating to a baby. And all of which also happen to be *safe* playthings.

Which brings us back to the safety factor, and I might as well take that up at this point. Sooner or later you will un- questionably be buying things specifically for your child to play with.

Certain things are—or certainly should be—clearly beyond the pale for the age group with which this book deals; that includes anything electrical, anything with sharp metal parts, anything made of hard plastic (which tends to get broken and display sharp edges), any target toys such as darts or bows and arrows, anything (such as a chemistry set) that re- quires the user to read and heed special precautions (ignore this one if your child is some sort of genius and has been read- ing and grasping complex notions since the age of three).

Beyond that, it may be informative to mention some cate- gories of toys which the BPS has seen fit to ban—not on whim, I assure you, but because something about them has previously proved to be extremely hazardous. Among the po- tentially damaging items:

● squeeze toys with easily removable squeakers (which are easily swallowed or aspirated);

● stuffed animals with button eyes that could be pried out by little fingers (and, similarly, swallowed or aspirated) or sharp wires used to stiffen ears (especially of rabbits), paws, or tails;

● mislabeled games meant for larger folks—such as lawn darts or sports-shooting implements sold in toy departments (darts are fine for kids if they're the suction-cup kind—but be sure that pulling off the rubber doesn't reveal a sharp metal tip);

● dolls with highly flammable clothing or hair, or straight pins used to secure hair or clothing, or sharp wires in arms and legs;

● balloons, horns, and other birthday-party favors containing small, removable noisemakers or mouthpieces that could conceivably be swallowed or aspirated;

● pull toys and rattles with swallowable small objects inside;

● tops with spinners that are sharp metal spikes, sometimes concealed by innocent-looking suction cups (which should be pulled off—as a tot can do—and looked under);

● toy cars with wheels that are easily pulled off, thus—like other tiny objects—possibly finding their way into tiny mouths;

● sharp edges, whether on metal or plastic toys, that could cut little fingers (among the banned items: cars and trucks, toy musical instruments, toy "tools," pull toys, tops; and it should be noted that metals and hard plastics, whether or not they *come* with sharp edges, can acquire them when they're broken).

You may feel that this doesn't seem to leave you much to choose from in the way of store-bought toys. Actually, it does. There are quite a few purveyed that don't fit in the dangerous, or potentially dangerous, category. Fortunately, the really lethal items are—at this writing, at least—in the minority.

Here are some noncomplex, nondangerous kinds of things you can buy for your youngster at various ages (which are very approximate, and necessarily extremely rough; peg your purchases to your own child's progress):

About 1: hanging toys; simple blocks; music boxes (that are not easily dismantled); sit-and-bounce gadgets (Jolly Jumper, etc.); peg-and-hole sets; box nests. *About 2:* stacking and nesting toys; moving toys (without sharp parts or removable wheels); mirrors and magnets; nontoxic crayons; water toys; a simple set of well-made blocks (which will not develop splinters, as cheaper blocks will) that can be added to as the child grows older (children play differently with blocks at different ages); the simplest jigsaws; dolls. *About 3:* put-together-and-take-apart toys; construction toys; toys and games using symbols, possibly letters and/or numbers; ball games; cloth- or plastic-coated books; finger paints; hand and finger puppets. *About 4:* well-made cars and trucks that won't come apart (Tonka is one excellent brand); chalk and blackboard; more complex construction toys; beginning board games (generally utilizing pictures rather than words); more advanced books and jigsaw puzzles.

All this is very generalized. And can't really be carried beyond this age. (I may even have stretched things with the "about 2" advice—which is, of course, also generalized. Your two-year-old may be at some totally different level.)

I would also add this, on the general subject of toys vis-à-vis the child of two, three, four, or five. As I suggested earlier, a toy is whatever turns a particular child on. Thus, whatever you are interested in can well be, or provide, toys for your child. And I happen to think that the parents' imagination may well provide the ultimate toys for any particular child.

If you play and/or have a piano, great; I have never known a child to whom this did not seem the perfect "toy" (and how could a two-year-old possibly harm a piano?). If you are a hobbyist or collector—well, you'd better wait until you're sure your particular offspring will not damage your prize specimens, but that may be earlier than you think (depending, of course, on the fragility of what you make or collect). Also note some further ideas at the end of Chapter 11 (pages 201–3).

In sum, there are two factors it's desirable for you to take into account: your child's potential, and his or her lack of experience. In the first area, you can—in my view—challenge your child all you like, although he or she certainly shouldn't be chastised if your hoped-for level hasn't been met (do remember that youngsters are totally unpredictable on an individual basis). In the second: it is up to you, and solely within your purview, to protect your child from the ever threatening hazards that surround him, from his toys or anywhere else.

10

Dealing with Doctors, Dentists, and Hospitals

I certainly assume your child will encounter at least one doctor, if only for the quite necessary checkups and vaccinations that are basic, and minimal, medical care.* I hope he will encounter a dentist within the range of years covered by this book. It is devoutly to be wished that, except for his initial, postpartum stay, hospitalization will not be necessary.

In all these areas, some basic guidance may be helpful. My aim—as it is throughout this book—is to make things easier for you, your child, and, in this case, the medical personnel with whom you may be dealing.

* Regular checkups should start at the age of one month; I personally generally recommend a once-a-month schedule for the first six months, then every two months until the age of a year, every three months until two years, semiannually thereafter—but follow your own doctor's preferences. Immunizations (again, follow your own doctor's advice, since opinions do differ) generally begin at two or three months with a DPT—diphtheria-pertussis (whooping cough)-tetanus—shot and a dose of OPV (oral polio vaccine). For further comment on my own recommendations, see my prior book (Appendix B); should you happen to get an early printing of that book: smallpox vaccinations are no longer considered routine—a decision made by the Public Health Service some two weeks after the book went to press. We authors have our troubles.

Doctor You Like, How to Find a

Obviously, you want to entrust your child's health only to someone on whom you can rely. Equally obviously, you want not only a duly qualified individual but someone who fills you with that nice, relaxed sense of feeling that you are in at least good, if not superb, hands. Someone you can *talk* to. Someone who *understands*. I am not making fun. I am serious. This is important.

Now, how do you go about finding that person? (I am of course assuming you are reading this book because you are— or are about to be—parents of a first child. If you already have a child, I hope that child has a regular doctor. But if you are moving, of course you are starting from scratch.)

I should explain at the outset that concepts of medical care have been changing rapidly in recent years. What you need in the way of doctors may depend a great deal upon (a) where you live and (b) what the customs are in your particular community. At this writing, it shapes up—roughly—this way. Chances are, if you live in a small place with few physicians, there will be few narrow specialists. The doctor who attends you may be a specialist in family practice—a physician not unlike the old "general practitioner," but one who has had special training in certain other areas, including internal medicine, obstetrics, pediatrics, and psychiatry. If that is the case, he or she will probably have been your doctor prior to and during pregnancy, will have delivered your baby, and will continue to tend to the medical needs of the new member of your family. A family physician is, incidentally, very much attuned to the other specialties, and quick to call in a consultant when that's indicated.

In a larger community, things get a bit more stratified. Chances are your own medical needs are met by an internist, and that your child's gestation was overseen by an obstetrician (or an obstetrician-gynecologist). Your challenge at this point, obviously, is to find a pediatrician. Internists deal only with grownups. OB-Gyn people deal only with sexually mature women, pregnant or otherwise.

Ideally, you should get a recommendation from someone who knows you pretty well. Most obstetricians know a number of pediatricians, so that's a good place to start; he or she is in a good position to know what sort of person you like to deal with (doctors, like engineers, dress designers, and politicians, remain individuals despite their special training, and there are many perfectly competent pediatricians who will not suit you as individuals). If you are now *expecting* your first child, this is an ideal time to choose your pediatrician.

A good source if you have recently moved may be your nearest neighbors who seem to have reasonably healthy, happy children. Should you observe such little folks playing about the neighborhood, inquire of their parents who has kept them in such fine condition. If you are about to move, talk to your present doctor, who may know of a colleague, or colleagues, in your new location.

Whatever your situation, try to get two or more recommendations from your source. This will save you some time, in case the first one doesn't work out.

Your first step is to take the first name on the list and call for an appointment. Be perfectly frank about the purpose of your call; the doctor you are phoning—or the nurse or receptionist, or whoever answers the phone—has absolutely no right to resent that purpose (if you get that feeling, forget it). Make an appointment for a talk with the doctor. There may or may not be a charge, and that is *not* a basis for acceptance or rejection. Although some doctors may not charge for such a visit, they are fully entitled to do so. A doctor's profession is purveying not goods but time and knowledge. If he or she is professionally qualified—and let us assume that your listed names are duly licensed—then a fee may properly be charged.

When you talk with the doctor, be as frank as possible about anything you feel may be relevant to the subject. If, for example, you and your spouse are vegetarians and you wish to raise your child that way, say so; if you spring it later, and your doctor disagrees violently, you are certainly going to run into serious trouble. If you are adamant about breast feeding, or adamantly against it, say so—and find out the doctor's views. If you know that some of your habits would not fit in with what you feel that doctor is accustomed to, be candid; he or she may feel uptight about attending a family of nudists, or commune-dwellers, or whatever idiosyncrasies may crop up (you've got to be realistic).

Look around the doctor's office while you're there. Observe the décor (do you feel comfortable?), the patients (do *they* look comfortable?), the parents of the patients (do they look *satisfied?*).

You have every right—and, in fact, an obligation to your child(ren)—to ask pertinent questions about your prospective doctor's qualifications and habits of practice. I noted earlier that I assumed he or she would be licensed; you should ask to see that license if it is not displayed (look around). Has he or she passed the special examinations ("Boards") in the specialty, be it family practice or pediatrics? (Again, a certificate may be in view—but if you don't see one, ask. A certificate will be headed American Board of whatever the specialty.) If the individual is described as "eligible," does that mean that the examinations will be taken very soon? (A certain amount of actual practice experience is required before the exams.) *Ask.* Is the doctor connected with a hospital—i.e., privileged to admit patients there? (He or she had better be.) If so, is it a hospital affiliated with a nearby medical school? (That's good.) Or, if not, is it a hospital that has a working relationship with a not too distant medical school? (Not bad. This means that the hospital has probably been accredited by the various specialty boards and has approved residency programs. Somebody other than the proprietors is judging the place.)

How about availability? Does this doctor make house calls? (Put it as a direct question.) If not personally—is there someone on call who does? You will want to feel that there is someone you can count on in an emergency. What happens when the doctor is out of the office? Who takes the calls? Who answers them?

You will also want to feel—especially if you are new parents—that there is someone you can call for a bit of advice, whether it's really an emergency or not. This is important, particularly for first-time parents. A good pediatrician or family physician is quite understanding about it and will patiently listen to the recitation of problems that simply don't occur the second time around. If you are fortunate enough to be sitting in the doctor's office when a call comes in, pay careful attention.

How does the doctor react to the call in the first place? If calls are refused when the nurse or assistant urges the doctor to take them—that should bring you up short. If the calls are accepted, how are they answered? Brusquely? Or in a concerned manner? Do you get the impression that the doctor cares more about the sick child or worried parent on the other end of the telephone line—or about you as a prospective new patient? You might ask yourself, if a call comes in while you're there: would you like to be on the other end?

Certainly what you are hoping for is an affinity, a rapport, a gut feeling that this is *your* kind of person. *Beyond* his or her professional qualifications. If the first doctor you talk to turns you off, or you're not sure, try another. It's perfectly all right to say, "We were given the names of three doctors, who were all very highly recommended, and we'd like to talk to the others before we make up our minds." If you can't find a physician whose personality truly delights you, then choose on the basis of qualifications.

There is one other item I haven't yet mentioned. One I find parents of new patients are unaccountably reluctant to mention. Money. Doctors do charge fees; they have to make a living, remember. Typically, there will not be too great a differential among physicians in the same specialty in the same area—although a doctor who is a diplomate of the appropriate board and spends part of his or her time instructing future physicians at the local medical school may feel, deservedly, entitled to charge a slightly higher fee than someone who has a license to practice, period. In any event, it is not out of line to ask the cost of various services—an office visit, a house call, a dose of polio vaccine, etc.

We're Off to See the Wizard

Visits to the physician's office could use some comment. Some parental preparation and foreknowledge can make things substantially easier for everyone concerned—child, parent, and doctor. I like to deal with relaxed patients and parents; my colleagues and I are not looking for any extra stress and strain in our own lives, either.

Your baby may or may not do any crying in the doctor's office during his first few months. If he does, it is not because he is frightened; rather, it is related to the discomfort of being undressed (the office may not be as warm as your own house), to sudden feelings of hunger, or to the momentary pain of injections.

At about five to eight months of age—rarely, as early as four months—babies start reacting emotionally to people and situations. They tend to evidence this, at first, by bursting into tearful screams at the sight of strangers and clinging fearfully to the nearest parent. This is not wholly a bad thing:

it means that they now know precisely who their parents are (which they didn't, before), have developed an attachment to them, and recognize and resent strangers. The recognition will persist; the resentment will not, once the youngster reaches what I call the "age of reason" (two or three years; it's variable), when he and the physician will be able to converse and he will be able to grasp what is going on. In the meantime, there may well be crying and resistance to examination. There may also be indignation: once the upright posture has been acquired, the child resents being forced to lie down.

Since you now understand why your previously softly cooing infant is carrying on so, there is no need to feel embarrassed or upset about it. Eventually, all will be sweetness and light. Meanwhile, there are several ways in which *you* can help to make things go a little more smoothly—or at least a little less traumatically.

Don't use the word "hurt" during one of these sessions, as in, "Does it hurt? Why is he crying, if it doesn't hurt?" or, "There, there, the doctor is just going to look in your throat, and it won't hurt." Of *course* it won't hurt. Don't suggest it by using the word. It will find its way into the child's growing vocabulary soon enough.

Don't feed the child just before the doctor's examination. It is very difficult to examine a throat obscured by a mouthful of apple, crushed carrots, or whatever. Recently fed tots are also prone to occasional vomiting all over the place—sometimes including the doctor and/or the parent—when they react to insertion of a tongue depressor.

Don't try to "help" the doctor by distracting the child with pleasant little noises; key-jingling is a particularly prevalent parental syndrome. It is hard enough to listen to a small child's heart and lung sounds—a vital part of any thorough examination—under relatively quiet circumstances.

If the doctor asks you to hold the child's hands, please,

preparatory to taking a close look at nose, throat, and ears—do so *firmly*, and hold those little hands down at the child's sides. This is chiefly to prevent the child's batting at the examining instruments; a jarred otoscope, in particular, can be damaging to your youngster's delicate ear canals, and quite painful.

Finally, if the doctor has indicated that the child should remain lying down, do *not* let the child sit up until the examination is completed. Sitting up repeatedly means pushing back down repeatedly, with louder and longer screaming.

After that "age of reason" I referred to arrives, you can enlist the child's cooperation in making physician visits more pleasant. At the same time, I would advise you to be careful what you say—and above all, *always be honest.*

This means, for one thing, that you should not tell a child that an injection "won't hurt a bit." Yes, it will hurt a bit—only for a second, true, but you can include that in your answer: "Yes, just for a second—but it will be over before you know it. I'm sure you're brave enough to stand the pain for that little bit of time."

There are fewer shots needed than there were in the past: smallpox vaccinations are no longer routine, and polio vaccine is usually given orally, so the main disease-preventing shots—assuming you are not leaving the country—are the one-time MMR (measles-mumps-rubella), usually given at about the age of a year, and the DPT (diphtheria-pertussis-tetanus), the latter usually a total of five shots given between the ages of two or three months and about three years. Oddly enough, children under five aren't as anxious about shots as older people are—and often don't turn their heads away as most of us adults do. It may bother *you* to see the needle going in; but if a child wants to look, let him (in fact, the child may become quite frantic if you forcibly avert his head).

By the same token, do not promise the child some prize ("If you're good, the doctor will give you a lollipop") unless you know for a fact that the doctor does have that in mind. Personally, I do not believe in dispensing sweets or other foods as rewards for good deportment; I think it can lead to undesirable habits, such as obsessive eating. Nor do I bestow balloons or any other awards; I do praise children for responsible behavior, and encourage parents to do so—but that's as far as I go. Your own doctor—and you—may have other ideas.

A positive thing you can do for the doctor is to remove the child's shoes as soon as you get into the examining room. Some youngsters have a mind to kick, and a three- or four-year-old can do so pretty forcefully; it's a lot less painful for both you and the doctor without the shoes.

You can also spare your child an annoyance by teaching mouth-opening for throat examination so that the tongue depressor needn't be used. Most children hate it, and I don't blame them; I've never liked having it used on me. The child should be taught to open his mouth wide, stick out his tongue, and to say *not* "ah," but "aaaaaagh"—something like a long-drawn-out version of the "a" in "bat." If this is done successfully, the mouth will be open far enough, and the tongue sufficiently out of the way, so that the nasty wooden stick needn't be used. Once you think your child can do this properly, clue the doctor in—if the child doesn't volunteer it—before a tongue depressor gets in there.

I would also advise you, when your child has reached this age of understanding, to keep an eye on the interchanges between doctor and child—and to pay attention to any opinion the youngster may volunteer about the doctor. Let me explain both admonitions.

It will be important—assuming your child continues with the same doctor through the childhood and teen years—that there be a degree of doctor-patient (and vice versa) communication. Now that the child is verbal, the doctor should be making an effort to establish that communication. I do not feel that a question such as, "What did Mary Lou have for breakfast today?"—directed to an accompanying parent— is appropriate if Mary Lou is perfectly capable of understanding and answering a direct question herself. By the same token, if Mary Lou directs a question to the doctor, it is helpful to listen for the answer. In the first place, there should *be* an answer. "What is that thing for?" or "Why do I have to have a shot?" or "How does that medicine taste?" should not be greeted with a stony silence. In the second place, the answer should be both informative (though, obviously, not a full medical lecture) and honest. Complex optical principles need not be outlined in explaining the purpose of an otoscope: "It lets me see way inside your ear so I can make sure everything is all right" is sufficient. "It tastes just like ice cream," on the other hand, is a terrible way to describe a teaspoonful of sheer nausea, and I don't advise child or parent to trust anyone who does so.

My second point is a little more subtle. If a youngster at least three years old declares adamantly, "I hate Dr. A———, and I don't wanna go there, and you can't make me," it may be well to query the child further rather than dismiss the complaint. If you ascertain that it was simply the DPT shot to which the child objects, assure him that that was the last one, or that only one more is needed (whatever is the case), explain the multiple ills it is designed to prevent, etc. And let him know that (a) you share his dislike of the experience and (b) the doctor does not wish to cause him pain either, but is simply bestowing protection against disease in the only possible way.

But if, despite your probing, Michael simply cannot explain why he has taken a dislike to Dr. A———, I would suggest that there may be something to it; there usually is. I would not automatically abandon the doctor; I would tell Michael, "We will go there one more time, and then we will see." Keep your eyes and ears open on that visit. Is there unnecessary (physical) roughness in handling the child during examination? Do you sense an unfriendly, unsympathetic atmosphere? Does the doctor ignore Michael's questions or comments? Or talk "over his head" as if he were not in the room? Or give him less than honest answers to questions? Or do anything else that makes Michael feel insecure or uncomfortable? (Including treating him as if he were two rather than four?)

It is, of course, up to you as the parent to judge whether the reason for Michael's aversion is serious or trivial (if it's something specific that the doctor can change, most doctors will do so), and whether or not a change of doctors may be desirable.

"Doctor, I Hate to Bother You, But . . ."

Sooner or later parents are faced with the do-we-call-or-don't-we dilemma. Typically, the problem arises at something like 4:00 A.M., when you are reasonably sure your doctor is fast asleep. Some reassurance is probably in order.

I think I speak for most pediatricians and family physicians when I say that I would much rather have a parent call me—at any time of the day or night—with a problem that eventually turns out to be trivial than not call about something I later find is quite serious and would have benefited from earlier attention.

As a general guideline, these are the things that can wait until morning and don't really merit disturbing your doctor in the wee hours: an ordinary cold (providing your child has had a cold before, and you're sure that's what it is); one loose stool; apparent constipation with no other symptoms whatever; one episode of vomiting; a rash that's the only symptom and doesn't seem to be causing any discomfort; and, obviously, anything—such as behavior problems or questions about future shots—that has no bearing on the child's well-being at that very moment.

Do call, whatever the hour, in case of: serious, or possibly serious, injury; any abdominal pain, especially if it's combined with loss of appetite (appendicitis, which if ignored can be life-threatening, is not uncommon in children over the age of two years); loss of consciousness, convulsion, or difficulty in breathing; a marked change for the worse in a child who is already ill (a rise in fever, for example); any discharge of anything—excepting the normal products of elimination—from any body opening; persistent diarrhea, vomiting, or both; persistent earache; fever of 103° F. (39.4° C.) orally or 104° F. (40° C.) rectally—or, in an infant who has never been ill before, 100.5° F. (38° C.); two or more unexplained symptoms, whatever they may be.

If, despite these overall guidelines, you find yourself in doubt, it is my own feeling that you should make the call. If *something* about that child's appearance, or the way he or she is acting (or not acting) bothers you, I think you should follow your instincts and pick up the phone.

A few words about phone calls, whatever the hour. For both your sake and mine.

Before you pick up the telephone, think for a moment about what the doctor will want to know. If Jimmy has fallen off a chair and is lying on the floor unconscious, obviously that is sufficient data. But "a pain in the abdomen" isn't. The doctor will want to know—because it's crucial—*where* in the abdomen, and for how long, and if it is continuous or intermittent, and whether or not there are any other symptoms (such as fever or diarrhea, for instance). Nor is "Susie feels kind of warm." *How* warm? Take her temperature. What else about her strikes you as being not quite right?

Have a pencil and paper handy before you place the call. Write, thereon, anything you think you might forget to ask once you get on the phone. Leave room for whatever the doctor may want to tell *you*. Have at the ready, too, your pharmacy's name and phone number—or, if it's the middle of the night, a pharmacy that's open around the clock (if yours isn't). Plus (check your medicine cabinet) any potentially relevant medication—previously prescribed for the same child (if you think it might be a repeat or continuation of a prior problem), or prescribed for another family member (if you think the child you're calling about might have caught something).

If you find yourself referred to another physician, be assured that your doctor—who is out of town or otherwise unavailable—has been very careful in selecting such a substitute. Write down the name and phone number, and use it.

If you must leave a message—i.e., if the doctor is not instantly available—state your problem and be as specific as possible. You may (depending upon the hour) encounter a nurse or assistant. Or you may have to leave a message with an answering service or a phone-answering device (do not be intimidated by the latter; they are frequently the most reliable relayers of messages). Make your message succinct and as explicit as possible (and if the answerer is a machine, mention the *time* of your call). The doctor—I know that in a crisis it's difficult to think of someone else's problems, but try—is going to have to decide which call to return first, second, and so on. "I think Marvin is sick" will not help a whole lot. (Why else would you have called?) "Marvin has a fever of 103° and funny pink spots on his face and left shoulder," or, "Marvin fell out of his tree house and he can't move his left hand" is a great deal more helpful. And don't forget to leave *your* name and phone number; your doctor may have seven small patients named Marvin.

I hasten to add that if Marvin—or Susie or Michael or Johnny—is in a state that seems to be life-threatening and requires *instant* care, you should call not your doctor but your community emergency number; rush the child to the hospital and call your doctor only after an emergency medical team has taken over. By this I mean any situation involving coma (unconsciousness from which you cannot rouse the child), uncontrollable hemorrhage, serious breathing impairment, or apparent heart malfunction.

If you are waiting for the doctor—whether your regular one or a substitute—to return a call, *stay off the phone.* Perhaps that's obvious. But many a physician has gone out of his or her mind trying to reach a parent who has left an urgent message, and then (a) repeatedly called back the doctor's office or (b) decided to pass the waiting time by confiding his or her anxieties to a friend or relative—thus generating a busy signal for incoming calls.

When you have the doctor on the phone, again get to the point as quickly as possible and state the problem as precisely as you can, so the doctor can assess the situation. Answer his or her questions as accurately as you can. *Write down* any instructions—for medication, for observation, for noting possible additional symptoms, etc. Be sure to write down any *numbers*; they are easily forgotten under stress. (Did the doctor say to call back and report Johnny's temperature at 10:00 or at 2:00? Was it one or two 1¼-grain aspirins you were to give him? What was that rectal temperature that would indicate some sort of crisis, and were you to call the doctor's number, or an ambulance, at that point?)

Finally: whatever the problem, if the child is old enough to talk and is able to talk—i.e., if his present condition does not prevent it—*put him on the phone.* If it is important to know precisely how Susie feels—and it often is important—there is no substitute for hearing Susie's own voice giving this information. Bear in mind, too, that if Susie is pretty sick, and needs treatment fast, your standing at the phone and relaying questions and answers back and forth when she can talk for herself is going to use up a lot of precious time.

Dentistry Is Better Than Ever

A lot of Americans, obviously, do not go to dentists. And equally obviously—and tragically—they are passing on their habits to their offspring. HEW's Children's Bureau has reported that fully half of all U.S. youngsters under the age of fifteen years have never been seen by a dentist. No one has surveyed the picture at the ages we are considering in this book. I shudder to think.

The fact is that your child should commence regular dental care at about three or four years. No, they are not permanent teeth. Yes, the baby teeth are going to fall out and be replaced by permanent teeth. But they are there because they are needed for chewing food in the meantime. And their premature loss can affect the positioning and viability of the permanent teeth. And—not least—it really is important to get into the going-to-the-dentist habit early.

We have, in this area, a problem of overcoming some prejudices. Many present-day parents grew up in an era—or perhaps a community—in which dental care was pretty primitive and pretty painful. That has all changed, radically. Dental techniques (and anesthetics) are better, and so are the methods of at-home dental care. I would suggest that, to start, you make a supreme effort to suppress any prejudices you yourself may have, as well as memories of severely traumatic dental experiences—because they're just not relevant any more.

There are specialists called pedodontists—dentists who concentrate exclusively upon dealing with children. There are, at this writing, very few such specialists, and they are relatively expensive. I would recommend your seeking out such a specialist if you have a great deal of money to spend

—or if you have a child who for some reason needs extensive dental care very early and poses special problems for the general dental practitioner. By and large, most children under five need only periodic checkups, some instruction by the dentist in brushing techniques, and possibly fluoride treatments. (Yes, brushing should start at about the age of two—with a kiddie-sized toothbrush, and *by the child*; your doing it might put too much pressure on the gums. And do use a stannous-fluoride toothpaste; such products *are* helpful in preventing decay.)

Certainly the best way to introduce the concept of dental care—assuming you are a good dental patient and you have a nice, gentle dentist—is to let your three- or four-year-old accompany you on one of *your* regular visits. Next, query your dentist as to whether he or she wants to take care of your child. All dentists have received training in dealing with children, but some choose not to treat them, and that is their privilege. If your own dentist prefers to limit his or her practice to older people, ask for a recommendation of a dentist who does deal with youngsters.

There is no reason for your child to think, on the first dental visits, that any pain will be involved, and don't give the child any such ideas. Don't even mention the word. Chances are those visits will entail no more than cleaning, periodic X rays, and some basic education in dental hygiene. If, incidentally, extensive dental work is needed—a rarity at this age—many dentists prefer to put the child under a general anesthetic (you may be referred to a dental surgeon) and do it all at one fell swoop, rather than subject the child to repeated sessions.

Hospitalization, Expected and Otherwise

You and I know that hospitals are great and marvelous places, accomplishing all sorts of curative miracles. You and

I also know that hospitals are huge, impersonal places populated by people dressed in white—all serious, all hurrying—and that they can be pretty scary places.

This will be especially true if your youngster is taken to the hospital for an acute, serious condition—e.g., appendicitis, a fracture, injuries incurred in an automobile accident, or some other emergency situation. An acute situation can, of course, be a minor one not necessarily requiring that the child stay in the hospital—a bad cut that needs a fast few stitches, for instance, or a minor arm fracture that is taken care of quickly in the emergency room and the child released.

In either case, however, the hospital visit is unexpected and generally everyone, including the child, is unnerved to one degree or another. The child will probably be very frightened (especially following an injury), and may be in severe pain as well. It is *vital* for the parent(s) to behave as calmly as possible in the circumstances. Let the medical personnel at the hospital take care of the physical problem; your role is to provide reassurance and support.

If possible—i.e., exclusive of an actual operating room—at least one parent should remain with the child *constantly*, and you should not let hospital personnel dissuade you from doing so. Doctors and nurses in the emergency room may request, or even demand, that you leave. *Don't.* Don't interfere or get in the doctors' way, of course—but stay there. (Make a scene if you must.) Your child *needs* your presence. Don't be afraid that you'll pass out, either (which may be what is motivating the people who are asking you to leave); parents will not faint when they know that their conscious presence is desperately needed by their child.

Predictable, planned hospital stays—for tonsillectomy or other elective surgery, or for diagnostic studies—are something else again. Such events should be discussed in depth with your child's doctor. Have him or her explain to you in detail exactly what will happen—not merely, "We'll take out Stephanie's tonsils and adenoids, and she'll be able to go home in a couple of days," or "I want to find out just what is causing Charlie's strange symptoms, and we'll need a few days of blood tests and other things"—but precisely what is going to occur from the time the child sets foot in the hospital. It's important for you to have full and accurate information—and for you to be able to explain things to the *child*, if he or she is old enough to seek or be offered explanations. And as I have cautioned before and will again: be honest with the youngster—including saying, "I don't know, but I'll try to find out," if that's the case.

Some pertinent topics: Will the procedure(s), or any part thereof, be at all painful? If there is going to be surgery, who will be in the operating room, and how will they be dressed? (Would *you* like to be suddenly surrounded by a bunch of giants wearing green masks and shining a spotlight on you?) Will there be premedication prior to the administration of a general anesthetic? (If so, what kind, and how will it be given, and what will be its effect?) Will there be pain when the child wakes up? Your physician may also have some suggestions on how to prepare the child for the experience.

Never, incidentally, use the word "sleep" to describe the child's state during an operation, as in, "They'll give you something to put you to sleep." "Sleep" is what the child does every night—and it is a poor idea to suggest an association of that everyday event with surgery. Rather, explain that "they will give you something so you won't feel anything, because they don't want it to hurt."

Of course at least one parent should try to be with the child as much as possible during the stay in the hospital (if there has been surgery, it is especially vital that the child see a familiar face upon awakening from the anesthesia); the youngster must not feel abandoned. Remember that small children have no sense of time, and that "Daddy will be here in an hour" does not mean anything to someone unfamiliar with clocks. A four-year-old may know what "tomorrow" means, since there's an awareness of the day-and-night sequence—but "next week" is something else.

There will be times, of course, when you cannot be present. Offer the nursing staff who will be caring for the child as much data as you can, to help them personalize their care: the youngster's special likes and dislikes, usual napping habits, any special family terms used for urination and defecation, etc. And if a child has a favorite toy or two that he or she is used to sleeping with, such items should go to the hospital too.

Children are usually remarkably cooperative with hospital procedures (such as the taking of blood from a vein for tests) *if* someone explains what is to be done and the reasons therefor, and tells the child exactly what is expected of *him*. (As this is written, I have a badly burned patient named Freddy. He is an extremely intelligent five-year-old. His major frustration, aside from the pain of his injuries, is that he has to go to great lengths to get people to tell him just what *he* is to do when they arrive—as they frequently do, and must—to take blood tests to determine whether his internal chemistry is holding firm through the necessary therapies.) Hopefully, the doctors, nurses, and other hospital personnel who attend your child *will* offer such explanations. If they do not, you should get the full story from them and, in turn, relay it to your child—*before* you permit them to go ahead with the procedure. Since the child is not old enough to speak up for himself, you should do that for him; that is one reason why you are there. Once the child does understand, he may continue to make a great deal of noise—but he will not thrash about and resist the procedure.

11

How to Stay on Your Feet When
You Have a Sick Child on Your Hands

Few things are quite so unsettling to a parent as the presence of an ill or immobile child in the house—and the extent of emotional upset is not necessarily related to the seriousness of the situation from a medical standpoint. Obviously, if you suspect some dire disease, you will take your child to the doctor and have it diagnosed. That's not where the difficulty lies; there, your course is clear-cut.

It is three other problems, in my observation, that can wear parents of young children to the point of frazzled collapse. Some prior practical knowledge about what needs to be done, what doesn't, and how to accomplish the former in the easiest and most effective manner may prevent your requiring intensive care by the time your youngster recovers.

Sneezes and Sniffles: Rx for URIs

They used to be known as catarrh or, among the more erudite, coryza. Doctors will sometimes describe them as an acute rhinitis—which pinpoints the initial site. More often, we label them Upper Respiratory Infections—URIs, for short.

Most people call them colds. They are, as everyone knows, very common and very contagious. And miserable. And inescapable. There's no proof at this point that vitamin C or anything else will prevent them, and there is nary a vaccine on the research horizon (so far, 113 distinct viruses that cause colds have been turned up; if you were to be inoculated with all of them at once, chances are you would wish you had an everyday cold).

Your children will, in short, have colds. They will have sneezes and sniffles, their noses will be by turns runny and stuffy, they will probably cough, they may run a low fever, and they will certainly feel generally rotten. No matter what miraculous nostrums you may see advertised, there is nothing that will cure a cold. I would urge you not to spend your money on any of those so-called "cold pills." They are invariably combinations of ingredients. It's quite true that some of those ingredients may be useful—but they're available all by themselves, far more cheaply. And certain other components of such patent medicines—the astonishing list includes antihistamines (which will be helpful only if there is also an allergy problem), laxatives, antacids, quinine, atropine, codeine, and more—may be either (a) useless, (b) harmful, or (c) both.

What you can and should do is, first, try to make the child more comfortable. The most useful agent for that purpose is simple aspirin, given in whatever dosage your doctor recommends. Minor throat irritation can be helped by steam inhalation or, if the child is old enough, sucking on hard candies; use cough medicines only if your doctor so suggests.

For nasal stuffiness, sneezing is great and shouldn't be stifled—and it is, in fact, the only way an *infant can* get rid of that mucus in there. An older child should be encouraged to blow his nose if he has learned how—which ability is extremely rare at the age of a year, still uncommon at two, and unmastered (or resisted) by many still older youngsters. A vaporizer or humidifier is also helpful to loosen up clogged nasal passages.

There are also nose drops and sprays. These should be used only if your doctor recommends them, and not otherwise. One frequently recommended is Neo-Synephrine in ¼ percent (children's) strength—but if your doctor specifies another, of course do as directed. I suggest you purchase it in a plastic spray bottle (see the advice on administration later in this chapter). Use it sparingly—and don't continue that use beyond the normal duration of the cold. For two reasons. One: the decongestants are fairly powerful drugs, acting not only on the nasal membranes but on the system generally (which is the reason to consult your doctor before using them in the first place; they shouldn't be used at all for some youngsters). The other: there is, after a time, a "rebound effect" that causes the nasal membranes to swell even more when the drug wears off—so that larger and more frequent dosages are needed, the congestion recurs to an even greater degree, and so on and on. These products are, I reemphasize, quite useful—on a short-term basis, and according to directions.

Secondly—in addition to comforting ministrations—be on the alert for complications and try to prevent them. Small children are especially susceptible to aftermaths, since their passages between the nose—basic trouble site of any cold— and the ears and the throat are shorter than those of larger people. Keep the child's resistance up by seeing that he gets plenty of nutritious liquids, such as soups and fruit juices (most small children will refuse solid foods when they are suffering from a bad cold)—and stays away from people who might be purveying other germs. A call to your doctor is in order if: a presumed cold persists for ten days or more (there may be a sinus infection); thick, yellow material is sneezed or blown out of the child's nose (signaling a probable secondary bacterial infection of either nose or sinuses, since mucus from an ordinary cold is clear); there is evident chest congestion; the child coughs all day, or there is severe throat pain (coughs in ordinary colds are simply efforts to clear material dripped from the back of the nose, and are most noticeable at night and early in the morning); the child has high fever, chills, chest pain, earache, or any other symptoms.

It Must Be Good, 'Cause It Tastes So Bad: Getting Medicine Down

Sooner or later you are going to be faced with the task of getting medicine of one sort or another into your child. The route of administration and the type of medicine may vary considerably.

Medicine is medicine. Obvious? Of course. Yet thousands of toddlers are poisoned because it is described as something else—candy, for example. And the other side of the con-the-kid coin is that if the youngster absolutely loathes the stuff he figures somebody has lied to him. Which they probably have. I never tell a child that a medicine that must enter his body through his mouth will taste good (most three- and four-year-olds will ask) unless I know for a fact that it does. If I know it doesn't, I say so; if I don't know, I say that too—but add, "It probably tastes awful, but I know you'll take it like a good sport, because it's going to make you feel better."

If you can communicate with a child verbally, tell him or her the truth. Including how the medicine is going to be administered, what it will accomplish, and—not least—that it *is* a medicine.

With some, though not all, systemic medications, there may be alternative forms and routes of administration: liquid, pills (capsules or tablets), suppositories, injection.

The choice may depend upon the age of the youngster, the site of the trouble for which the medication is being given —and the child's own feelings; in cases where a child is old enough to understand, and two or more methods are available, I discuss the alternatives and give the child a choice. This makes things a lot calmer and easier for the child, the parents, and me, since, if they have made the choice themselves, children are often extraordinarily cooperative.

I am reminded of Nancy, age four, a very determined young lady who had always refused oral medication of any kind. She came in to see me with two badly infected ears, for which an antibiotic was needed. She told me calmly that she wasn't going to take any pills or liquids. I said, equally calmly, that then I had no choice but to give her the medicine by injection—and I warned her that four or five injections might be needed. She said okay, she'd rather have the injections. That's what we did—and she took every shot without a murmur, much to her parents' (and my) amazement.

A few months later Nancy again had an infection that brought her to my office. This time, however, after I ascertained that she again required an antibiotic, she burst into tears and cried, "I don't want any shots!" Fine, I said, but again, the medicine was absolutely necessary, and she would then have to take it by mouth. Her reply: "I'll think about it all the day, and I'll think about it all the night, and tomorrow I'll take the medicine." I agreed, even though Nancy's mother was a little anxious about postponing therapy for at least eighteen hours. But I had faith in my little friend. Sure enough, the following day she advised her mother that she was prepared to take the prescribed medication by mouth— and proceeded to do so. When she returned to my office for a follow-up visit, she proudly announced, "I'm a good medicine-taker now! No more shots!"

Injections have their advantages and disadvantages. They

are used (aside from immunizations and for fast emergency administrations, such as adrenalin in anaphylactic shock, or antivenin for a snakebite) chiefly for antibiotics. One advantage is that the doctor knows the medicine has been given in the proper dosage. Another is that it can be administered despite the patient's inability (or refusal) to swallow oral medication. But allergic reactions are apt to be more severe. Often the injections must be repeated daily, or even more frequently—which is a nuisance for all concerned. And they hurt, sometimes quite a lot—which doesn't make for a happy patient or a happy doctor-patient relationship.

I like to reserve therapeutic injections for those children who are vomiting or for some other reason cannot swallow or retain an oral medication, and for those who—like Nancy—refuse oral medication or whose parents are reluctant to force oral medicine upon them (which must sometimes be done; more about that a bit later). In those instances, I will choose one of the antibiotics less likely to provoke an allergic reaction than, for example, penicillin. And I give the injection in the arm; I've found that youngsters universally object to injections in the thigh or buttock.

Antibiotics require some additional specific comment. We prescribe (or administer) antibiotics only when, in our judgment, they are necessary either therapeutically or prophylactically; and with a handful of exceptions, they are ineffective against viruses, so in general are used essentially for bacterial infections. One reason they are used sparingly is that they sometimes tend both to stimulate resistant bacterial strains and—true more of some drugs than of others—to act indiscriminately against innocent, non-disease-producing organisms. The second major reason is that, with many of the most useful antibiotics, there is the possibility of what are loosely termed "side effects." Allergic reactions, as noted, have occurred—as have a variety of difficulties either more or less serious. For these reasons, your doctor considers very carefully before prescribing an antibiotic for your youngster.

You, too, have certain responsibilities, both negative and positive. Don't exceed the dosage—or period of medication —your doctor has specified. Do, on the other hand, continue the medication for *as long as* specified; one of the peculiarities of antibiotics is that they tend to banish obvious symptoms very quickly—while the infectious organisms sit quietly waiting in the wings, ready to pounce the moment the drug is discontinued.

Additionally, you should watch for any adverse effects. Some such developments could, of course, be symptoms of the ailment being treated—and it is not necessarily possible for you to tell the difference. Without being specific, I would make it a general rule that if *anything* new—be it as mild as a slight stomach upset—occurs while your youngster is taking an antibiotic, you report it to your doctor without delay; he or she will know whether it is an expected concomitant of the child's illness or an adverse effect of the medication, and will advise you what (if anything) to do.

If you discover, through bitter experience, that your child has an allergy to one or another of the antibiotics, it is imperative to so advise any physician or dentist who is treating that child—at once, the moment you begin taking the child to that doctor. As I've mentioned, one of the most prevalent allergies is to penicillin. In addition to the natural forms of this drug, there are newer, semisynthetic forms; they are sold by many trade names. *All* major trade names contain some part of the word "penicillin"—i.e., "pen," "cil," or "lin" (Amcill, Omnipen, Prostaphlin, Totacillin are examples). This is one of the reasons that I always direct pharmacists to label prescription containers with the name of the drug (both trade and generic, if both apply). Should you discover that your child is allergic to penicillin, certainly in the first place inform your doctor—or any *new* doctor you patronize. And be alert to what has been prescribed. If you spy one of those key syllables in the name of a drug, whether a generic name (those all end in "cillin") or a trade name—and you know your child is allergic to penicillin—get on the phone and get a substitute prescription, fast.

There is, incidentally, a fairly new group of antibiotics called cephalosporin derivatives. Trade names include Kafocin, Keflex, Keflin, and Loridine. I mention this because in some individuals a *crossover allergy* between the penicillins and this group has cropped up—so that if your youngster has been found to be allergic to penicillin you should beware of these drugs as well.

A third major group of antibiotics are the tetracyclines, termed "broad-spectrum" drugs because they are effective against a wide range of ailments, including not only many caused by bacteria but the major rickettsial diseases (Rocky Mountain spotted fever is the one most prevalent in the U.S.) and even a few viral infections as well, including psittacosis (parrot fever) and viral pneumonia. Tetracycline itself is perhaps better known by trade names such as Achromycin, Robitet, Steclin, Sumycin, Tetracyn, Tetrex; other members of the family (all their generic names end in "cycline") include Aureomycin, Declomycin, Minocin, Rondomycin, Terramycin, and Vibramycin.

We try to avoid giving the tetracyclines to children under the age of seven or eight, if we possibly can. In a very few young children, these drugs can affect developing teeth (teeth that have already formed, even though they have not yet erupted) so that when they appear they are stained bright yellow—a condition otherwise harmless, but certainly not desirable. And obviously least desirable if they are permanent teeth at the front of the mouth. This possibility is well known to pediatricians—so be assured that if yours has prescribed one of these drugs it's because it's essential.

There are two other possible transitory side effects. Some of this group, notably Aureomycin and Terramycin, tend to cause slight but uncomfortable intestinal upsets—a result of the drugs' sweeping antibacterial action, which can temporarily upset the normal balance of harmless bacteria in that area; such reactions may be minimized by giving yoghurt along with the medication. Secondly, the tetracyclines increase sun sensitivity in some people, resulting in painful burns even from brief exposure—so that it's best, just to be on the safe side, to keep the child out of the sun while the drug is being taken.

Aspirin is undoubtedly the medicine you will be called upon to get into your youngster most often; it is also the leading cause of poisoning in under-five children, on which more comment elsewhere (see the index). It comes in many forms. There are regular adult aspirin (5-grain tablets and less generally available capsules); children's aspirin (flavored, generally 1¼-grain tablets, although some are made in 2½-grain strength); suppositories, which come in various sizes ranging from 2 to 10 grains; and time-release tablets, which I do not ever recommend giving to young children.

(I would like to note, in passing, that your doctor's recommendation of aspirin means just that. It does not mean "buffered" aspirin, or "extra strength" aspirin, or a "combination of ingredients" product—usually aspirin plus caffeine, sometimes with another less effective or potentially toxic ingredient thrown in. None of these things, despite what their makers claim, is any more effective, faster-acting, or less likely to upset the stomach than aspirin—which is highly unlikely to upset a young child's stomach in any event; if your child does evidence any slight upset, it can be minimized by giving the aspirin following a meal—or with a full eight ounces of water. Nor does it mean a misleadingly named liquid product called Liquiprin—which is not aspirin at all, but quite another analgesic, acetaminophen; this is a useful drug, particularly in adults who have a demonstrated sensitivity to aspirin, and for whom it is available in tablet form under other trade names. Acetaminophen does not create the sense of well-being that aspirin does; nor is it effective against inflammation, which aspirin is.)

Aspirin is probably the closest thing to a "miracle" or "wonder" drug that we have in the pharmacopoeia. It (1) lowers fever, (2) relieves mild to moderate pain, (3) reduces inflammation, and (4) acts in a sense as a mild, ephemeral "tranquilizer," generally minimizing discomfort and promoting a feeling of well-being. Because it does do these things, on the other hand, it shouldn't be given to your child *without* your physician's recommendation. If three-year-old Rosemary is feeling terrible, and you give her aspirin and then call your doctor an hour or two later, you might have suppressed—or, as we say, "masked"—what may be the crucial symptoms; Rosemary's rash may be quite evident, since aspirin will not banish it, but other significant manifestations of the particular illness may be temporarily absent. Thus you will have done your doctor a distinct disservice, making it much more difficult to arrive at a correct diagnosis.

As a general rule of thumb, aspirin dosage is one grain per year of age every four hours—which is why ten years old is the usual cut-off date for children's aspirin. A five-year-old's dose would thus be a single adult tablet (or four 1¼-grain, or two 2½-grain, children's tablets). But check it out with your own doctor—or with some doctor—if at all possible. In certain instances your child may require an altogether different amount. If a child fails to respond, whatever the dosage used, consult your doctor before repeating.

The easiest way to administer aspirin to an infant is to crumble the tablet and put it on top of a teaspoon of solid food. Or dissolve it in a little water and drop it into the child's mouth with a dropper. (See, too, the further comments on infant medication later in this chapter.) An older child may go along with gumming or chewing up a whole (children's) tablet; they do dissolve pretty readily, once they get into the mouth. If you happen to have a child like one I know, you might try throwing the tablet on the coffee table or the floor. One patient of mine, Harold (the name has been changed to protect the eccentric), is known to be intensely attracted to anything strange reposing either on the floor or on normally out-of-bounds adult furniture, and his parents have found that he will eagerly ingest anything, including medication, left there.

Sometimes aspirin in suppository form is a recommended resort. It is certainly preferable to fighting with a feverish, cranky child who may refuse the medication simply because he or she feels miserable. Often, I've found, such a child may be perfectly agreeable to taking a subsequent oral medication—another dose of aspirin, an antibiotic, or whatever may be prescribed or recommended—once the initial dose of aspirin has made the child feel better. (See, a bit later, some special advice about suppositories.) In a pinch, an ordinary (uncoated) aspirin tablet can be used as a suppository—but it is not so designed, it may be quite irritating, and calls for the use of a lot of lubricant (e.g., petroleum jelly).

If a child will swallow aspirin—i.e., uncoated tablets—you might try to get him or her to swallow them unflavored. You can always *add* flavor in the form of the accompanying liquid. When the dosage is, say, two baby (1¼-grain) tablets—bear in mind that this adds up to half the standard adult tablet. *Break an adult tablet in half* and give it with orange juice. You will save a great deal of money this way. You will have fewer bottles in your medicine cabinet. Always try to uncomplicate things.

I noted earlier that aspirin holds the unenviable number one position as a poisoner of youngsters—due, in great part, to (a) the pleasant flavoring of aspirin designed for children and (b) adults' referring to medications as "candy." Not to mention (c) the fact that little children ingest all sorts of things—including detergents and floor waxes—that you and I would consider inedible. By the time you read this, I am hopeful that the statistics may have begun to change.*

Oral administration is the typical route for most medications. Tiny babies aside (see the separate hints about them, page 193), most small children are not happy about swallowing pills. Therefore, a good number of medications designed for them are available in the U.S. and Canada in liquid form. Flavorings are often included, in a commendable effort to make these liquids more palatable—an effort that is sometimes successful, sometimes not, and may vary with the tastes of the individual child. Typically, your pediatrician will try to make the taking of medication as pleasant as possible under the particular circumstances.

It is for this reason that your doctor is likely to prescribe a brand name rather than a generic—or may give you samples of two or three different brands of the same drug (equally effective, but differently flavored) with instructions to try two doses of one, then two of another, etc., and that you should note your youngster's responses. (Which means, of course—as I have said before in another connection—that all prescriptions should be fully labeled as to the brand and identity of the medication; this is a good general rule anyway, for safety reasons.) If Susie gags on Company A's penicillin preparation (or asthma medication or cough syrup), but gets

---

* Since January 1973 the FDA has required safety packaging for aspirin and products containing it—defined as packaging (be it box, bottle, or other container) that a sampling of children under five cannot open 85 percent of the time, but that a panel of adults *can* open 90 percent of the time. If you have any aspirin in your house that is not so packaged, I urge you to keep it under lock and key.

down Company B's or C's with no trouble, remember it and remind your doctor when next that kind of medicine is needed.

Measurements for liquid medications must be accurate. "One half teaspoon" does *not* mean an estimated-by-eye fraction of what you stir your coffee with. "Two drops" means precisely that. Most households do have a set of measuring spoons in tablespoon, teaspoon, half-teaspoon and quarter-teaspoon sizes; if you don't, you should. A standard medicine dropper is also useful; get your doctor (who may have samples) to give you one, or buy one from your friendly neighborhood pharmacist. One of the drug companies that manufactures antibiotics for children supplies, along with its fruit-flavored product, a very handy test-tube-like gadget with a spoon-shaped top, calibrated to measure half-teaspoon, one-teaspoon and two-teaspoon doses (if you need a larger dose, remember that three teaspoons add up to one tablespoon); I find this just about the easiest way to dispense liquid medication—and the children enjoy the novelty, too. This device, called a Flexidose spoon, is also available at some retail drugstores.

Flexibility, patience, and resourcefulness are the overall parental qualities needed for getting necessary oral medication into a child. Each child, and each situation, is different. Some needed liquids are *not* pleasantly flavored and have a taste everyone agrees is disgusting. Others may be available in a choice of cherry, orange, and lime flavors—which takes care of most people's preferences, but *your* four-year-old may absolutely detest any and *all* fruit flavors. Certain medications are made by only one company and in only one form—which means that's the one that must be used and there just isn't any choice. In short, from time to time there is going to be a problem. Knowing that the medicine must get into the child somehow, an open mind about the method will be helpful.

The first solution, of course, is a different form or flavor; if your youngster is balking at getting the medicine down, immediately inquire of your physician if an alternate product is available. If it's a bad-tasting liquid that's bothering the child, you might suggest a switch to pills. I have had some patients as young as three who have learned to swallow pills or capsules, simply because they hated the taste of the liquid medications. Pills can, of course, be washed down with water, milk, or whatever the youngster happens to like—fruit juice, soda, etc. Some children of three or four can even swallow coated pills and capsules without liquid. And any oral medication can be followed by a fast "chaser," which often helps.

I mentioned resourcefulness earlier. I once had a patient named Eric. Eric's trouble happened to be a worm infestation (yes, they do happen sometimes), for which the only available medication was a pill. Eric simply could not swallow a pill. Eric's parents were at their wits' end—and so, as a matter of fact, was I. But Eric's father got a really brilliant idea: he gave each pill a thick coating of butter, then put them in the freezer. From that point on, those pills went down into Eric's gut as smoothly as . . .

What if you simply cannot think of any way of getting a balky youngster to take medication—if *every* offer of medicine, in any form, gets a violent, hysterical reaction? In that case, there is no other recourse: the medication must be *force-fed*. This is a last-resort measure, and one that should be limited to children at least two years of age. It may sound barbaric. But I can tell you that it works. Here's how:

You will need two people. Both should wear old clothes or large plastic aprons, because it is not improbable that the child will vomit all over you. Person number one: hold the child on your lap with his back to you and his legs between your legs, so he cannot move them; wrap one arm around the upper part of the child's body, including his arms, and hold him tightly to you; with the other hand, hold the child's nose (so he'll have to open his mouth in order to breathe) and tip his head back slightly. Person number two: with one hand, pull the child's lower jaw down so his mouth is open widely; with the other, spoon or drop the medicine in, as far back as possible. Then immediately close the child's mouth. Wait for him to swallow. As soon as he does, let go of his nose. If he spits out the medicine or vomits, start over.

Yes, it does sound barbaric. But really, it is sometimes—though happily not often—needed. I would like to emphasize that *you must not evidence anger:* the force-feeding must not be interpreted as an act of vengeance or of punishment. Tell the child calmly before you use this method that it is very important that he take the medicine and that if he will not cooperate you simply have no choice but to use force, although you would prefer not to. He is ill, you love him too much to want to see him sick, and the medicine is needed to make him better. When the whole scene is over, tell him—again, calmly—how sorry you were that it was necessary, and assure him that the unpleasantness will not be repeated if he will cooperate when the next dose is due. One such experience is usually enough; the odds are that he will readily take the medication next time.

Small babies of course can't swallow pills; you've got to use liquid. One easy way to get medicine (or vitamins) into an infant is with an eye dropper. Get a moderately large one from your druggist—plastic, not glass. You can also get from the druggist a small medicine glass marked off in half-teaspoon doses. Pour the medicine from the bottle into the little measuring container, then draw it into the dropper. Open the baby's mouth and drop the medicine fairly far back on the tongue, so it will be swallowed reflexly; if you put it on the tip of the tongue, the child's reflex action will be to spit it out. Empty the dropper slowly, so the baby can swallow a little at a time.

Another convenient route for baby medication is via his bottle. Put the prescribed dose into the bottle, then dilute it with no more than an ounce of water, milk, or juice (ask your doctor to suggest the most suitable vehicle for the particular medication). Give it to the baby *before* his feeding. After he has taken it, add a little more liquid to the bottle and feed him that, just to make sure that all the medication gets into him. Then proceed with his regular feeding.

Nose drops present a particular problem, because all children hate them; I have never known one who didn't. (The upright spraying that works for older youngsters and adults generally isn't useful for under-fivers, because they can't get the knack of sniffing the spray up into their noses.) But they're sometimes needed. I suggest that, rather than drops per se, you get one of the plastic spray bottles that contains the same kind of decongestant (see the earlier comments on page 181); turned upside down, it does dispense drops—and further, it's unbreakable, and, unlike a bottle with a dropper, takes only one hand to use. Makes life easier all around.

A four- or five-year-old, despite his loathing of the stuff, may cooperate. Simply have him lie down on his back; no pillow beneath his head, of course. Don't bother to count individual drops. Just squeeze once into each nostril. If the liquid runs down his face, repeat; it has to get into his *nose*. If he sputters or complains that he can taste the stuff at the back of his mouth, and it's *terrible*, that's fine; it means it went through his nasal passages.

And if nose drops have been prescribed and the child won't lie there nicely and quietly while you administer them, but persists in jerking his head back and forth and bobbing up and down, so that every time you think you've got good aim at a nostril you end up squirting his eyebrow? Then you'll have to *make* him immobile long enough to get the drops in. First, if he is wearing shoes, take them off; this is to protect *you*, in case he kicks. Then—let us assume you are right-handed—position the child on his back, with his head to your left. Grab both his wrists with your left hand and extend his arms over his head; you will find that his arms are now held tightly against his ears and he cannot turn his head. Lean across the upper part of his body, resting your right elbow on the bed or table (the spray bottle is in your right hand), and administer the drops. (If you're left-handed, of course, reverse things.)

Don't exceed your doctor's recommended frequency and duration of use for nose drops; again, see my comments on page 181.

Ear drops are something else you may be called upon to administer at one time or another. Precisely how to do it depends upon what they have been prescribed for. Begin, in any event, by positioning the child on his side with the affected ear upward.

If there is an infection in the outer ear—a condition medically termed otitis externa, and popularly known as "swimmer's ear" because that's often how it's contracted—be very, very gentle; this condition can be quite painful if the ear is even lightly touched. Try not to pull or tug on the ear. Simply drop the medication in until the ear canal is filled. Then —again, very gently—put a plug of absorbent cotton at the outside so the medicine won't run out when the child sits up. Use a *large* wad of cotton, leaving most of it outside (i.e., don't try to push it into the canal); it is preferable that the cotton be lost outside the ear, not inside. Leave the cotton there until it drops out, the child pulls it out, or the next dose is due, whichever occurs first.

For a middle-ear infection (otitis media), proceed similarly, except that you need not be leery about touching the ear; there's no external pain. Pull the ear out gently, then drop in the prescribed amount of medication, and again, add a wad of cotton.

If you're dripping some peroxide in to loosen wax prior to removal by your doctor, of course there's no pain involved whatever. And no cotton plug is needed.

It's helpful to warm ear drops slightly, by holding the bottle under the hot-water tap, before you administer the medication. Most children are *very* irritated by something cold being dropped into an ear. (And never store ear drops in the refrigerator; not only will they get too cold, but many will congeal.)

Eye drops or other eye medications are very difficult to administer; I sometimes wonder if these or nose drops would get the most-hated vote if a poll were taken among preschoolers. I wouldn't want to wager on either.

Generally when eye medication is required it is because the eye(s) is/are infected. There is inflammation, there may be pain, and the child is pretty uncomfortable. Then he gets assaulted by someone trying to inflict something into that sore area. His typical response—violent resistance—is understandable. Nevertheless, the medicine has got to get in there. Like the administration of nose drops to an unwilling youngster, administration of eye medicine requires immobilizing the child—and it's done in the same way, by laying the child on his back and pressing his elbows against his ears to keep his head still. Unlike nose-drop instillation, this is a two-person job. The child's head really must be *completely* immobile; otherwise the medicine will not get in—and there is the danger, too, of poking the child in the eye.

Once one person has gotten the child immobilized, the other puts the prescribed medication in as instructed, holding the eye wide open with the other hand. If it's a liquid, drop it into the lower lid (pull the lid down as far as you can); if you've gotten it into that lid, don't worry if some of it trickles down the child's face. If it's an ointment, use a little more than you actually need; when the child closes his eye (with either liquid or ointment, he will automatically blink), rub your finger tip gently over the closed eye to smear the stuff around—then wipe off any excess around the eye.

Do not be surprised if, after you have applied an ointment, the child blinks, opens his eyes, and screams. It is because there is a film over his eye and he is momentarily blinded. You would be scared too. Naturally, if the child is old enough, it is helpful to forewarn him—and assure him that the condition is purely temporary and will go away in just a minute.

A child with a chronic eye problem—a muscle difficulty, for instance—that requires long-term medication will generally get used to receiving the medication and will not struggle like a youngster with an infection. Even an eighteen-month-old—though he may not be overjoyed—will often be fairly cooperative. His eyes, after all, are not sore. In such a situation, after you've used the above procedure a few times, you'll probably be able to handle it with just one person, like the nose-drops instillation.

Suppositories may be prescribed either when that's judged a viable route for systemic medication (aspirin is available in this form), or if the trouble is specifically in that area. The advice I am about to give you may seem either elementary or obvious, but it is here because all sorts of silly mistakes have been made, so bear with me.

Keep the suppositories in your refrigerator, in a clearly labeled container; you do not want anyone supposing they are oddly shaped after-dinner mints. Take them out one by one, as you need them, about an hour before the scheduled insertion. Suppositories are designed to melt once they get inside the body—but room heat can affect them as well; the one hour isn't long enough for melting but will soften the suppository sufficiently to make for fast absorption after it's inserted.

Most, though not all, suppositories come wrapped in foil; remember to remove that foil—or whatever else it may be wrapped in—before you insert it. Most, though not all, suppositories are differently shaped at the two ends; if that is the case with the one you are using, it is the rounded end, not the straight one, that goes in first. Most, though not all, suppositories require the use of petroleum jelly prior to insertion; if there are no instructions to the contrary, assume that is the case with the one you are using. The easiest thing to do is to dip the suppository into the jar so it really gets a good, greasy coating (remove the wrapper before you dip it into the jar). Some suppositories require water, and if that is the case, there will be instructions to that effect; check the wrapper.

When you insert the suppository, shove it as far up into the rectum as you can, by giving it a firm push with your finger (if you meet resistance instantly, right at the anus, there is a stool ready to come out; let the child defecate, *then* insert the suppository). Then quickly squeeze the child's buttocks together and hold them that way for five minutes by the clock; three to five minutes is needed for the suppository to melt fully. If the child has a bowel movement immediately following that, just check the stool to see if it contains any parts of the suppository; if you can't see any, you can assume the medication was absorbed.

Bed Rest, the Doctor Says

If you are filled with dread at the thought of trying to keep three-year-old Tommy—who under normal circumstances rarely *sits* in the same place for more than five minutes at a time—resting contentedly in his bed, you might consider that "rest" does not necessarily mean *bed* rest. Just because you've been advised that Tommy should refrain from his usual frenetic activities for a few days, this needn't mean you must confine him to his bed—or even to his room.

Before you panic, make a point of pinning the doctor down to specifics. An in-depth discussion can clarify just what degree—and duration—of rest is necessary. And can avoid a good deal of needless work, aggravation, and exhaustion on your part. Ask your doctor to spell out just what is permitted and what is not. Does he or she, for example, really mean Tommy must lie flat on his back? May he sit up—in bed or elsewhere? How about going to the bathroom? If lying down is what's called for, might the living-room couch provide a change of scene?

Most common childhood ills do not require bed rest, though a good deal depends on how the child feels; if a youngster really feels pretty sick, he may choose to remain in bed for a couple of days, until he feels better. Fever, per se—even a fairly high one—is not necessarily a reason to confine a child to bed. There are a few conditions in which we generally do insist upon prolonged bed rest, because it is part of the therapy; most such ills—including hepatitis, acute nephritis (a kidney infection), and acute rheumatic fever—are fortunately uncommon among preschoolers. And of course a fracture or other disabling injury will restrict a child —whether to bed or not, depending on the nature of the problem; if Tommy's problem is a broken leg, it's obviously of little consequence where he sits or lies, and all that's needed is someone to carry him from one room to another.

Once you have established the degree and duration of activity restriction—be it strict bed rest or some other, less drastic measure—you can key your coping to the situation.

Namely: how do you get that child to (a) accept the prescribed restriction, (b) do so with a certain amount of con-
tentment, and (c) permit you to function in a manner that
will not send *you* into a state of collapse the moment the
youngster is up and around?

No real problem is going to arise with a youngster who
feels rotten. But a child who feels perfectly capable of going
outdoors and making mud pies, or racing up and down the
stairs twenty times a day, will not accept with grace a direc-
tive to remain quietly in bed or in a chair. Nor will a child
clearly curbed in his activities (by, say, a broken leg, which
is hardly arguable) simply shrug his shoulders and resign
himself to the inevitable; he is inclined to become restless,
annoyed with himself and annoying to you, and often un-
bearable. Remember that the average child under five cannot
read and does not enjoy the interests of an older youngster
—who might be consoled with popular music, books, cross-
word puzzles, correspondence, and the like. A small child's
recreations are typically purely physical. Kind of makes you
feel sorry for him, doesn't it?

Now that I have struck that note of sympathy, I must warn
you that a sick, but not critically sick, youngster is very easily
spoiled. Parents, being generally kind people, sometimes tend
to become so concerned about the child's very real frustration that the sick youngster quickly becomes king or queen
of the household and the parents of both sexes are reduced
to the role of handmaidens. You do owe some time and
thought to your other children if you have other children, to
your spouse, and—above all—to yourself.

First of all, get the doctor's directions very clear in your
own mind. Make them as clear as you can to the child. (Don't
make any attempt, though, to specify time limits if they are
either indefinite, dependent upon future developments, or
lengthy. Children of this age have little or no concept of

time, and "The doctor says you must rest for six weeks" will be meaningless.) And refuse to argue them or discuss them further. They are medical imperatives, like getting medicine down when it has been prescribed, and are not to be questioned (not by the child, certainly).

Then, within the context of the child's condition, devote a little thought to ways in which you can keep him relatively happy and out of your hair. The following suggestions may lead you to some ideas of your own.

A child who must lie in bed needs—and deserves—a little more parental time than one who can be a bit more active, or at least sit up. It's pretty hard to play games with someone who's flat on his back. But he can be read to—not only by you but by an older brother or sister as well.

He can also be entertained by TV. And by "shows" put on for his benefit by siblings and/or friends. And by film or slide projections on the ceiling or high on the wall, so he can see them without lifting his head from his pillow.

If a child needn't really be in bed at all, but must sit still, certainly let him do some of his sitting at the kitchen table, or in the living room, or—if it's warm weather, and your doctor permits it—in the back yard. A youngster who is, understandably, bored to tears sitting in the same bed all day, and is likely to start jumping up and down on said bed (so much for the *rest*), will often be perfectly content to sit quietly coloring pictures at the kitchen table.

For a youngster who can sit up—in bed or elsewhere—there are a host of possible pastimes. If you have wanted to introduce some quiet and/or creative activities into his life, and you'd heretofore been unable to catch him on the run, here is your golden opportunity. Simple card games and board games designed for his age group, for instance—to be played with parent or sibling. But it's smart to put the emphasis on things that will keep the child occupied by himself for substantial periods of time. Picture books, certainly. A new stuffed animal, or a doll with which he can "play doctor." There are generally available, too, many attractive but easy-to-do jigsaw puzzles that are great for preschoolers. If you're buying the invalid some new playthings, by the way, do be considerate, and don't give him things he's unable to use because of his disability. That admonition shouldn't be needed, and generally isn't needed for parents themselves—but well-intentioned relatives and friends have been known to present a child who has a broken leg with a brand-new scooter "so you can get well fast and use it." (How would *you* feel?)

Not that you need deluge the child with store-bought stuff. Crayons—or even pencils—and a generous pile of scrap paper will keep a child occupied for an astonishing length of time (and the resultant creations can—and should—be displayed to the family at the end of the day). Toys can be made by the child himself—things for stringing, for example, which include not only beads but spools, buttons, and macaroni as well; *un*stringing and *re*stringing make for infinite variations. Old magazines and a pair of kindergarten-style scissors can provide endless delights. (Encourage the child to make up—and later tell you—"stories" involving people and scenes selected for clipping.) You can even enlist the child's aid in chores: while sorting and pairing socks (or checking for holes, or whatever) may be dreary work for you, it can be a new and interesting game for a four-year-old.

Finally, this personal note. If you can obtain an old, discarded telephone, do so. I have two such phones in my office waiting room—one attached to a wall at child level, the other sitting on a table. They are, of course, not connected to anything at all. But they are in constant use. And they are wonderful examples of the extraordinary scope of children's imagination. As I came out of my examining room the other day, chatting with one of my teen-age patients, I overheard the following conversation.

BARBARA (*age almost four, earnestly, into the wall phone*): Yes, and after we leave here, we're going out to lunch. (*Pause.*) No. (*Pause.*) I don't know. I'll see. (*Turning to her sister, who is leafing through a picture book at a low table.*) Daddy wants to talk to you.

CAROL (*age almost five, annoyed*): I can't. Tell him I'm reading a book.

BARBARA (*into the phone*): She says she can't, she's reading a book. (*Pause.*) All right. (*Turning to Carol.*) He says he wants to talk to you.

CAROL (*exasperated*): I ca-a-a-an't! Tell him I'm *busy!* And I'll see him later.

BARBARA (*into the phone*): She says she can't, she's busy. (*Pause.*) Okay. (*Pause.*) Okay. G'by. (*Hangs up phone, turns to Carol.*) He says okay.

Yes, true. Try it.

If you can't get hold of an old phone somewhere (you might try the local telephone company), you could unplug a plug-in phone if you have one, and let your invalid make calls to his heart's content. But don't let him take it apart; Mother Bell wouldn't like that.

12

I Am Curious (Toddler)—Or,
How to Cope with Sticky Sex Questions

A good deal of what your children do—and say—in this area is going to surprise you. I say that with assurance, because I am sure you will not remember that you in all likelihood did and said the very same sort of things when you were small. Try to retain your cool at all times. And be advised that it all begins well before the toddler stage.

It's Hard to Believe, But Babies Do It Too

I am talking about masturbation. Yes, they do. Practically all of them. Many begin as early as the age of six months; some have been known to start as early as two or three months. The timing depends upon when the individual infant happens to discover that the activity gives him or her pleasure.

A boy may begin when his exploring hands happen to encounter his penis, he plays with it, and it feels good—so he plays with it some more. A girl may find her clitoris in the same way, or she might be impelled to finger her vulva if she's afflicted with pinworms (which are very common; the worms emerge at night to lay eggs around the anus, they sometimes wander to the vagina, and their presence causes itching), finds it pleasurable, and continues after the infestation has been banished. Either sex might be turned on initially just in the process of being bathed, or while rubbing against their clothing.

In any case, once they discover the pleasure of the sensation, they will do it deliberately; sometimes they will even have orgasms (although small boys, of course, cannot ejaculate). It will not harm them in any way, physically or mentally. Many people are extremely uptight about masturbation because of the sea of misleading information that has been disseminated in the past—and is unfortunately still being disseminated, in some sectors of our society, today. Despite what you may have been told to the contrary, masturbation will *not* cause memory loss, visual impairment, mental illness, future sexual problems, acne, or anything else. It is in no sense a perversion; nor is it a "bad habit" of which a child should be "broken." It is a normal human activity.

As youngsters grow into toddlerhood they often develop— or, more accurately, discover—subtler sources of sexual pleasure that are acceptable in public, reserving direct genital stimulation for private moments; the former include tricycle seats, swings, slides, seesaws, and the like. Boys of four or five may engage in mutual masturbation with friends (girls are unlikely to do so until adolescence, and it is rare even then)—again not a harmful practice if they are of the same age (something pretty peculiar is going on if one partner is a fifteen-year-old).

I hope I have convinced you that masturbation is not something you should be the least concerned about. I realize, though, that this knowledge will not necessarily enable you to discard, overnight, prejudices and old wives' tales that may have been inflicted upon you earlier; all I can say is, *try*.

Mothers are often, for some reason, more upset than fathers are when they discover that their children (of either sex) masturbate.

The mother of one of my patients once received, in this regard, an illuminating insight. "Jimmy," she asked her four-year-old exasperatedly one day, "must you play with your penis so much?" Jimmy looked at her thoughtfully and answered, "Mommy, you're just saying that because you don't have one!" It took her a moment to recover, at which point she suggested, "Well, I would rather you do it privately."

Which is, of course, the answer. It *is* a private matter, like using the bathroom. Not "dirty" or "shameful," but private.

Once a child begins to play outdoors, as I mentioned, direct genital stimulation *will* probably be reserved for private moments at home; just before falling asleep is a favorite time. If you notice the youngster masturbating during the day, and it annoys you as any repetitive habit might, you might suggest an immediate something to do with his hands, whether a task or a play activity—*without* making any reference to the masturbation (simply, "Georgie, how about helping me sort these socks"—not, "Stop that this minute, Georgie, and sort these socks instead").

If a child spends a good many daytime hours masturbating, there *is* something wrong—but not with the child. Children do masturbate a great deal more when they are bored, tired, or unhappy; it is, after all, a pleasant, time-consuming, ultimately relaxing activity. I suggest, if this is happening, that you look for reasons for the child's boredom, fatigue, or unhappiness—and make some effort to provide the child with some other interests. Masturbation does not become a preoccupation if there are other pleasant things in a child's life.

Vive la Différence, Right?

Gender awareness may prove a disconcerting development.

It typically dawns on a child about the age of two or three that there are two different sorts of people in this world. That thought often leads to intense curiosity about the *other* one, one's *own* classification having been ascertained.

This curiosity is often directed at a sibling (or playmate, if there is no sibling) of the opposite sex, and frequently takes the form of wanting to watch the other child urinate. Should this be permitted? you might wonder. I don't think you will have any choice; children generally manage to arrange these things between themselves. Once their curiosity has been satisfied, and they've witnessed the event two or three times, they are not going to insist upon hanging around every time the other child makes a trip to the bathroom.

But you may, at this point, be assaulted with a few queries, mainly centering about the obvious anatomical difference, and beginning with "Why?" Certainly the earliest "Why doesn't *she* have—" and "Why don't *I* have—" questions can and should be answered as simply as possible: "Because you're a boy and she's a girl" (or vice versa, if that's the case).

Psychologists worry a lot about the child's going on to theorize that her penis was stolen (if the child is a girl) or that his penis may be subsequently lost (if it's a boy)—thus creating considerable anxiety. I haven't found that this is generally true. A child may well, however, press you further as to why boys have penises and girls do not. I think you can probably get away with something along the lines of, "It's just one of several differences between boys and girls. These differences don't really mean much now, but when you grow up they will. Girls grow up to be women, and they can also be mommies. Boys grow up to be men, and they can also be daddies. You'll see, when you grow up."

If, of course, you have already been into a fairly advanced explanation of the baby-making process, you can be a little more explicit. Which brings us to *that* subject.

Inside Stuff

Questions about the origin of babies are something you are certainly going to be confronted with if you have one child—or more than one—and are expecting another. A youngest child may not become interested in this topic until a bit later, unless there is a pregnant friend or neighbor in evidence. (See, for further comment on timing of telling an older sibling the news, pages 134–35.)

There are two consistent facts of which parents should be aware, in order to spare themselves headaches and other psychosomatic sequelae.

One is that, as I've noted earlier in this book, children are quite literal. A child asking what chairs and tables are made of is not requesting an in-depth thesis on the furniture industry. So it is with this subject. *Listen carefully to the child's question and answer what has been asked.*

The second is that, for reasons unknown, children *repeat* questions to which they have already received answers. Not instantly, but perhaps days, weeks, or months later.

I do advise you to be honest, in dealing with this subject as with any other. I hope and trust you will not thoroughly confuse your child by feeding him or her tales of big white birds swooping down to deposit babies on doorsteps (today's child might sooner accept a helicopter). I also advise you, because of that repetition factor, to be *consistent;* the child repeating a question may have forgotten the answer—or he may be looking for confirmation.

Here follow some common questions—your child may phrase them somewhat differently—and my suggested answers, which of course must be modified to respond to the particular query your child has posed. Though I have arbitrarily organized them into a hypothetical "conversation," they are not in fact likely to be posed all on the same occasion, and certainly not necessarily in the same order. Typically, a child will ponder the answer to one or two questions, then return—either on the same day or at some later date—and pursue the subject further. (Or start all over again!)

Q. "Why are you (or, is Mommy) getting so fat?"

A. "Because a baby is growing inside me (or her)."

Q. "*Where* inside you (or her)?"

A. "In a special place called a uterus, that mommies have." (*Don't* say it's in the stomach, or belly, or anything else the child is aware that he or she possesses.)

Q. "Is it a boy or a girl?"

A. Answer truthfully. If you don't know, say so. If by chance you have, for another purpose, had embryonic cell sampling done, and you know what the baby's sex will be, say so.

Q. "How big is it?"

A. "When it's ready to be born, it will be about" (visually demonstrate a length or height of about nineteen or twenty inches—the average height of a newborn). "Right now, it's still growing, and it's only about *this* long." (Average lengths of the developing fetus: at two months, about an inch; at three months, about three inches; at four months, about eight inches; at five months, about ten inches; at six, about one foot; at seven, about fourteen inches; at eight, about a foot and a half.)

Q. "How will it get out?"

A. "When it is time for it to be born, it will start to push its way out, and the doctor will help."

Q. "But *where* does it come out?" (Whether the child says so or not, the belly button and the anus are prime possibilities in his or her mind.)

A. "From a special place mommies have, called a vagina. Not the same places urine or bowel movements" (or whatever you call those, in your family) "come from."

Q. (This is the really sticky one.) "How did it get there?"

A. "Mommies have a tiny, tiny seed that joins with another tiny seed from the daddy, and together they make a baby."

Q. "How come *daddies* don't have babies?"

A. "Because that's what makes them daddies, and not mommies. Mommies are the ones where the babies grow."

Q. "Will *I* have babies when I grow up?"

A. Obviously, the answer depends on the sex of the child. If a girl: "Yes, you will be able to; you'll have that special place for a baby to grow." If a boy: "No, boys grow up to be daddies, but not mommies."

Q. "How did Daddy's seed get inside you?" (Or, "How did you get your seed inside Mommy?")

A. (Obviously, with appropriate personal pronouns.) "Daddy's penis goes into a special opening in Mommy and releases the seed." (If you're asked *what* opening, be specific; *say* it's the vagina.)

Q. (From a boy.) "Can *I* make babies in you (or, in Mommy)?"

A. "No, you have to be grown up to make babies. And of course there will be somebody else who will be the mommy of *your* children."

Q. "Can I watch you and Daddy (or Mommy) next time you make a baby?"

A. "No, that's a private thing, between Mommy and Daddy."

Q. "Can I see where the baby will come out?"

A. "No, because there isn't really anything to see until the baby's *ready* to come out."

Q. "Can I watch *then*?"

A. "No, I'm afraid not. I (or Mommy) will be going to the hospital when that happens, so the doctor can help me (or her) and the baby, and nobody else is allowed to get in the way, because it's very important." (Or, if the father is planning to be present at the birth, "—and they don't allow children to be there, because all the grownups will be very busy, and children might get in the way.")

Q. "Can I see the place where Daddy (or you) put the seed in you (or Mommy)?"

A. If the questioner is a boy: "No, it's a special part just for daddies to use." (As I said in the Introduction to this book, you are getting my views. If you wish to show your son your—or your wife's—vagina, that's your business.) If the questioner is a girl: "It's the same as this place *you* have" (showing her hers). "But you have to be grown up before you can have a baby."

Q. (From a girl, following the last question.) "Why?"

A. "Because little boys and girls can't make babies. That only happens when you are more grown up."

Q. "Do you have to be married to have a baby?"

A. (As I said, I do not think you should lie. Ever.) "No, but it's better that way, because then the baby has a family, both a mommy and a daddy, to take care of him or her."

Q. "Do babies start growing every time Daddy puts his penis in Mommy's vagina?" (Likely to come from a youngster who is somehow aware that sexual intercourse is not a one-time thing. Or perhaps is just speculating.)

A. "No, only if they are lucky. Sometimes Daddy's seed and Mommy's seed don't get together." (If your contraceptive method failed, I do not think it desirable to bring that up.)

Q. "How come Mr. and Mrs. Jones don't have any babies?"

A. You will have to play this one according to ear and your beliefs. If you know that Mr. and Mrs. Jones have some problem and would like to have a child, you can indicate that— i.e., that they "hope" to do so. If, on the other hand, you happen to know that the Joneses have no intention of ever producing offspring, and have taken extensive precautions to that effect, I do not think you should say otherwise; the Joneses are not going to be elated about your child's subsequent expressions of misplaced sympathy. You might suggest that some people are busy with other things and do not feel they have time to take care of a baby; if it's appropriate, you might cite the activities of Mr. and/or Mrs. Jones. If you *don't* know how come, just say so.

Q. "Did it hurt you (or Mommy) when I was born?"

A. "Why do you ask that?" (Obviously, nothing you have stated has intimated that. It's well to get the child's source of information—and how much "hurt" was reportedly involved—before you answer.)

Q. The child's statement at this point will probably refer to something he or she has overheard, perhaps relating to a "rough" or "difficult" time, or to consistent pain in childbirth.

A. If you are the child's father, I think it would be well to refer the question to the mother ("I don't think so, but why don't you ask Mommy?"). If you are the mother, an appropriate answer might be (I don't think it's very wise to use the word "pain"): "No, not at all." Or (if it was indeed rough): "No, not really. When a baby is born, he (or she) pushes hard to get out. The mother has to work, too, to help. Sometimes it's pretty hard work, but I wouldn't call it hurting; it's just a little uncomfortable for a while—you know, like when you have to do some hard work, like carrying something heavy. And I was so glad to see you when you were born that I forgot all about the hard work, anyway."

The foregoing may or may not cover the interrogatory ground *your* child has staked out. For further help, I refer you to two excellent sources of guidelines listed in Appendix B, the books by Ms. Gruenberg and Dr. Salk.

Nudity vs. Prudity (or, Nudery vs. Prudery)

Most experts in child care, including psychiatrists and psychologists, agree that after infancy it is not a good idea to make a habit of parading around nude in your child's presence—especially, though not only, a child of the opposite sex. While children should become familiar with the bodily appearances of others—of both sexes—it is best for them to acquire this knowledge by exposure to siblings and other youngsters of their own approximate age in a state of undress.

There are, basically, two reasons.

One concerns the parent of the *same* sex. The body of an adult is vastly different from that of a small child. Breasts, of course, are present in the adult female (and are perfectly evident even when she is fully clothed), but there are other, less obvious, differences as well: a young boy's penis and testicles (in fact even a ten-year-old boy's penis and testicles) are much smaller, in relation to the rest of his body, than his father's; overall body proportions are dissimilar, in both sexes; distribution of body hair—again, in both sexes—differs greatly. These differences may be confusing, and even frightening, to a youngster, since he or she often tends to compare his own body with others'; the comparing is best done with people of the same age and stage of development.

Secondly, extensive and/or frequent viewing of the nude body of the parent of the *opposite* sex can create some thoroughly undesirable psychological effects. Typically, such effects are delayed ones; your two- or three-year-old is hardly likely to make sexual advances to you. But these experiences may reemerge into the child's consciousness when he or she is in the process of achieving sexual maturity—and they can then create confusion in his or her attitudes toward, and relationships with, the opposite sex.

I do not mean, of course, that you should go into a state of acute panic if your child happens to walk in upon you and glimpse part—or even all—of your anatomy while you are dressing or bathing. Your youngster, at this point, is perfectly aware that one must take clothes off in order to put others on, and that clothing is removed for bathing purposes. You should not act coy or otherwise seductive or "sexy," either. Simply behave naturally and continue with your dressing, undressing, soaping, toweling, or whatever you are doing. The bodily revelation in such a situation is simply an incidental event and completely acceptable—unless *you* make it otherwise.

13

Thumb Sucking, Hair Pulling, Head Banging and Other Strange and Annoying Habits

Rare is the child who does not develop at least one distinctly irksome habit (irksome to his parents, not to him; he obviously does whatever he is doing because he feels he must, because he enjoys it, or at least because he is not aware of any viable alternative that will provide him with the same gratification). In this chapter I shall suggest reasons for that behavior, as well as alternatives.

In general, I would urge you not to pounce upon your thumb sucker, nail biter, or hair puller and cry, "*Stop* that, this *instant!*" Habits—as any adult will admit if he or she is being honest—are not that easily broken. The child who is so accosted, if the habit fills an emotional need, is likely to lie awake half the night making up for his daytime deprivation, so that the only thing you have accomplished is to tire him out. In some instances, in fact, he may be totally incapable of abandoning the habit, because it stems from some physical problem. And in some cases the habit may be deliberate, designed to attract attention; your agitation thus becomes a reward and encouragement.

Blanket Carrying (the "Linus Syndrome")

Many children—like Lucy's little brother Linus, the appealingly assertive tyke in Charles Schulz's "Peanuts" comic strip —develop an inordinate attachment to some object, which they carry about constantly. It is always something soft, usually something from their beds; typically it is indeed a blanket or quilt. They do this, even as Linus does, because it signifies security to them. They are not sick, and they do not need psychiatric assistance. They simply need help in abandoning the habit—which, basically, they want to do. But it can't be done cold turkey.

There is a practically guaranteed cure.

Approach Johnny and his blanket, at some point, and say, "Johnny, that blanket of yours is getting very dirty. I will have to put it in the wash" (or send it to the cleaner, or whatever). He will refuse to give it up. At this point, of course, it is serving no useful purpose for *you.* So you shrug, take out your shears, cut it in half, and say, "Well, at least I'll clean part of it." That won't disturb him in the least; he still has something to hang onto.

This approach can be repeated until the fragment of quilt or blanket Johnny is constantly clutching has shrunk to a two-inch square. By this time he is going to realize that the whole thing is pretty silly; you will soon find the remnant abandoned.

Hair Pulling

This habit can be one of the most aggravating ever, not because the action itself is disturbing but because the damage the child perpetrates can be so horrendous. It is no picnic for a parent to have the only half-bald child on the block. (If your youngster tugs out clumps of hair but still looks perfectly normal, your problem is very minor.)

There is no sure cure for this malady, and we frankly do not know what causes it. We do know that every child who does it eventually stops doing it and that there are no discernible ill effects afterward. Essentially, what you need is patience, based on the sure knowledge that the habit will not persist forever.

While it obtains, I would suggest a couple of practical approaches.

One is to keep the child's hair as un-grab-able as possible. Cut it fairly short; short hair is a lot harder to grab by the fistful than long hair. You might also try to encourage (though it may not work) pride of appearance by incorporating ribbons and the like into the child's hairdos.

Secondly, you might make a substitute available. One couple I know weathered the storm by providing a succession of toys—chiefly long-haired dolls, but including fuzzy animals as well—and encouraging the child to do the pulling that way. Obviously, it is best to precede this with a simple statement: you are aware of the habit, you are unhappy with the child's resultant appearance, and you hope that he or she—now being aware of your feelings—will subsequently utilize the toy for hair-pulling purposes. There will be a lot of bald dolls and animals before it all ends.

Sometimes, by the way, hair pulling is fairly transparently (to an adult, not to the child) an attention-getting device. It may disappear when the youngster lights upon another method of attracting adult concern.

Head Banging

This activity, which can be very frightening to a parent, sometimes occurs toward the end of the baby's first year. Typically, the head is repeatedly banged against the side or end of the crib, in a steady, regular rhythm. No one knows what causes an infant to carry on in this manner; we do know that it does not typically denote any illness, either mental or physical. It is possible that the child simply likes the rhythm of it—or perhaps it functions as some sort of tension reliever, as thumb sucking often does.

It is not, at any rate, a cause for alarm; though children may keep at it long enough and hard enough to cause some bruises or rub off some hair, they seem to know enough to stop short of really serious injury, which is practically unheard of. Nevertheless, to be on the safe side and to spare the child even minor injury, I think it's a good idea to put padding or quilting around the sides and ends of the crib.

Generally, head banging doesn't persist very long; only rarely does it continue until the age of two or three years —and then, often because the parents have carried on about it, and what began as a self-contained activity has become an attention-getting mechanism. So don't make a fuss; be assured that it will eventually stop, whether you do anything about it or not. In the meantime, if it is making you very nervous, there are some things you might try, although I do not promise that any will work for your child.

One is synchronizing a metronome to the tempo of the child's banging and placing it near the crib. Another is to tune a radio to an all-music station and place that in the child's room; try, when you first turn it on, to select music in a tempo that approximates, as closely as possible, that of the child's activity. Sometimes the ticking of the metronome or the beat of the music seems to satisfy the baby, and the head banging ceases—for that night, at least.

You might try giving the child a bath immediately before bedtime. Sometimes the activity in the bath will have the effect of relaxing the child, and he or she will go quietly to sleep.

If the banging is loud enough to disturb the neighbors—

i.e., in a thin-walled apartment house—you might also move the crib away from the wall. Or have the child sleep in a play-pen or other place close to the floor, for a while.

If none of these measures work, and the banging is driving you up the wall, you might discuss with your doctor the possibility of a mild sedative—for you, the baby, or both.

Lip Biting (or Sucking)

Typically, the lip biter attacks his or her lower lip, and doesn't do so constantly; it's generally reserved for moments of anxiety or confusion. Actually, there are two problems.

One is that the lip itself can well become terribly sore and may even bleed. Since the child's mouth is open in order to attack the lip, the lip is also very dry from being breathed upon—which makes the problem worse. It is not, however, a really serious problem. Certainly make it a point—the moment you become aware of the habit—to apply soothing anti-chap ointment to the tortured lip, which will help it to withstand the irritation.

Having done that, do call the habit to the child's attention —quietly and calmly. Very often the child is simply not aware of what has been causing his or her physical discomfort (of which there *is* awareness), and the enlightenment will prove a completely effective answer.

Nail Biting

As you are doubtless aware, nail biting is a very widespread habit (though less common in this age group than in older children); if you bite your nails, it is going to be very difficult to persuade your offspring that it is an ugly and loathsome habit. If you do not, it is still going to be hard to stop. It is particularly subject to the problem I mentioned at the beginning of this chapter; *nagging* a nail biter *never* helps.

What you can or should do depends on both the cause and the child himself. Nail biting typically stems from tension— but may also arise from boredom or be related to definite emotional disturbance (in the latter case, other habits or symptoms will often be evident too).

Generally speaking, you might make a point of trying to relieve any special tension the youngster may be under. You might also encourage his getting involved in some new and interesting activities necessitating the use of his hands. I don't think material rewards for ceasing the practice are advisable; presenting a child with a prize for not doing something you don't want him to do can suggest the desirability of his thinking up *other* distasteful activities he might be bribed to stop.

If the nail biting persists despite your efforts—especially if there *are* other signs of tension or emotional upset—talk it over with your pediatrician or family doctor.

Nose Picking

Don't be horrified if your child picks his nose; it's very common in small children. Don't even be surprised if, after doing so, he pops his finger in his mouth; that's not uncommon either. I agree that it is a pretty disgusting habit. Fortunately, children are generally more responsive to requests to stop than they are with some other habits. Try not to show your feelings of repulsion. Simply present him with a tissue and show him where they are kept. Point out that "we all get dirt in our noses. When it bothers us, and we have to take it out, we use a tissue, not our fingers, and then we throw the tissue away, like this. Next time, that's the way *you* should do it *too*." There are likely to be occasional lapses, but he will learn.

"Not Nice" Language

Somewhere around the age of four, if your youngster attends nursery school or socializes with other children of the same age, he may come home and begin to spout a string of socially unacceptable language—what I call "bathroom talk." Suddenly everything and everyone undesirable, or at which or whom he is angry, becomes a "B.M.," a "shit," a "turd," or whatever your family word is for that material or process ("You're a *duty!*").

Don't get too disturbed; this is a normal phase of development. Without making too much of a fuss, just tell the child you prefer that other words be used to express his feelings.

If a child also comes home with some other generally unacceptable four-letter words—i.e., sexual street terms—that he has not heard in your house (if he has, you'll know where he learned them), again, don't get angry or wash his mouth out with soap. Don't act shocked or giggle either; if you react that way the first time he tries out such a word, don't be surprised if he continues to use it just to create the same effect.

What I suggest you do is ask him if he knows what that word means. Usually you will find that he has not the remotest idea of its meaning. Enlighten him, or not, as you see fit. And point out to him, calmly but firmly, that the word "is not used in our home."

Pacifier Persistence

Earlier, I spelled out what is in my view the proper use—and *im*proper use—of a pacifier (pages 18–20). If you've proceeded along those lines, your youngster will not stroll down the street with a pacifier in his mouth. Even if you haven't, a child is aware enough, by the age of two or three, of how children generally behave in public—and of peer pressure not to "act like a baby"—not to do it. If he does insist on using a pacifier in public at the age of three, simply point out that he is not a baby any more and tell him you will not permit him to use the pacifier in public.

It is not going to hurt your child to continue to use a pacifier to help him fall asleep, even if he is three or four years old. He is not clinging to infantile behavior, merely to something that relieves tensions and helps to relax him; I wouldn't worry about it at all. You *should* be concerned, however, if it continues much *after* that, since the pacifier can push his permanent teeth out of line if the habit continues after they begin to arrive, which may be as early as age five (pressure on the baby teeth has no lasting effects). If you are having trouble persuading the child to give it up at *that* point, talk to your dentist, who may have some helpful suggestions.

Penis Clutching

By this term I do *not* mean masturbation, a universal practice I've talked about in the preceding chapter. Penis clutching is quite a different phenomenon; it is not, in fact, a sexually related habit at all.

Typically, the child will simply *hold* his penis—as opposed to rubbing or manipulating it—and his doing so is not related in any way to mood, time of day, privacy or lack of it (as masturbation often is): he may, in fact, be simultaneously involved in some other activity. Possibly there has also been apparent inability to achieve enough control to sleep through the night without bed wetting.

The problem is probably physical. See your doctor. Often, penis clutching is a symptom of meatal stenosis. "Stenosis" means the constriction, or abnormal narrowness, of a passageway; the meatus is the outer opening of the urethra, the passage from the bladder through which urine is excreted.

Meatal stenosis can be corrected surgically (the procedure is called a meatotomy), and that takes care of the problem.

Pica (Nonfood Nibbling)

Pica is still, to a great extent, a medical mystery. Sometimes the child may be seeking to compensate for some nutritional deficiency—either in his diet or because of some physical inability to utilize certain nutrients. In other instances, it is apparently a habit that has persisted since infancy (when most children will put practically anything in their mouths), and may suggest some emotional disturbance. There may be still other causes, and there is ongoing research.

The habit, in any event, involves continual eating of substances that are generally considered inedible—paint, plaster, dust, paper, fabrics. Often pica is highly selective; while one child may seek out chips of paint, another may confine his nonfood nibbling to strands of wool plucked from blankets, and still another to soil from the back yard.

Some of the things chosen for these activities are innocuous. Many are not—including, as you may know, paint and plaster, which are prominent causes of lead poisoning; statistically, some three in ten children who exhibit pica have been found to suffer from lead poisoning.

Pica is a self-limited phenomenon; it generally does not persist beyond the age of five. But whatever substance it is the child has chosen to consume, he should be seen by a physician without delay in order to determine the cause if possible, and to check for any damage the ingested materials may have caused.

Rocking and Rolling

These, like head banging (page 217), are medically classed as "rhythmic motor habits." Rocking or rolling of the child's

head generally appears, if it is going to appear, quite early—
perhaps when the baby is only two or three months old.
Rhythmic rocking of the whole body, like head banging, is a
later phenomenon.

I have the same suggestions here as for dealing with head
banging. You may be driven to desperate straits sooner with
whole-body rocking, since a really vigorous rocker can actually
shatter his crib—and, if you live in a thin-walled apartment,
can cause enough commotion in the course of his exertions
to drive not only his parents but the neighbors crazy.

Sniffling

Not much can be done about sniffling in a *very* small child,
except trying to relieve the cause of his stuffy or runny nose,
generally either a cold (see pages 179–82) or an allergy (if
you suspect the latter, your doctor is the person to see).
Babies and toddlers sniffle because they have not yet learned
to blow their noses. A youngster who has frequent colds is
going to do a lot of sniffling.

You can try to teach nose blowing as early as possible, but
I warn you that it's practically always impossible for a child
under the age of two years; the child who can learn it even
at two is extremely rare. Many children resist blowing their
noses for a long, long time, and there's little you can do about
it.

"Stuttering"

At the age of three or four "stuttering" is quite common,
and *perfectly normal*—i.e., not a true speech impediment;
generally, it means nothing more than that the child is in a
hurry and he can't keep up with his own thoughts (or hasn't
yet acquired the vocabulary to do so). It does not indicate
any kind of psychological disturbance or maladjustment.

More boys than girls have this difficulty, although we have no idea why; girls just seem to master language skills (as well as some others) earlier than boys do.

I must urge patience upon you. In *every instance* the child will outgrow it—*if it is ignored.* Meaning: *don't mention it.* Certainly don't make the mistake of calling attention to it in front of others, or permit others to mention it in front of the child. *Nor* should you: compare the child unfavorably with a more articulate sibling; interrupt him when he is talking, or otherwise evidence impatience (which will only create anxiety); punish him for stuttering or promise a reward for stopping it; offer gratuitous suggestions such as "Now, take a deep breath," or "You must speak more slowly"; permit siblings to tease him.

If you do make a "case" out of this perfectly normal temporary difficulty, you *can* create a problem; real stutterers are made, not born.

On the positive side: when the child speaks, simply listen attentively, encouraging him by indicating understanding at intervals ("Yes," or "I see," or whatever—or simply nodding). When the child produces an entire sentence without hesitation, evidence your pleasure by smiling warmly (not by saying, "Hey, you said a whole sentence without stuttering!"). Spell out your delight, in so many words, at any obvious verbal achievement, such as learning—and correctly pronouncing—a brand-new word.

If you find a further speech problem that is not answered by this advice, then you should talk it over with your doctor.

Talking to Imaginary Playmates

This situation may upset you dreadfully. Let me reassure you. A young child's carrying on a conversation with a person (or animal) that exists solely in his or her imagination is not evidence of schizophrenia or any other mental illness. It indicates, on the contrary, simply a vivid imagination—and is perfectly normal in young children of average or above-average intelligence.

Occasionally this behavior results from emotional deprivation: i.e., the child seeks in his or her imagination the companionship that is not present in real life—so it might be a good idea to question yourself on that score. But if the child relates perfectly well to real people, and the imaginary companion is simply an addition, you have a child with a great sense of make-believe. Which is, I think, an asset, in these troubled times; it is too bad that so many adults lose it when they grow up.

Teeth Grinding

This habit, known technically as bruxism, does not usually signal an emotional disturbance. In adults, it might; but not in small children. Typically, it will occur when the child is either preoccupied or asleep. Older children generally evidence this habit as a result of malocclusion—i.e., an improper "bite." But with the age group we are discussing, it is usually a "discovery" phenomenon: the child is playing with a new toy—a new part of his body. Once he gets accustomed to the "toy," the habit will probably stop. But if he or she has had a full set of baby teeth for some time, and the habit nevertheless continues, you might discuss the question with your dentist.

Thumb Sucking

Some babies require more sucking activities than others. Sooner or later they will discover one of their thumbs, try it, find it gratifying, and stick with it; while some such children can be persuaded to switch to a pacifier, some cannot, and continue to insist upon that thumb and nothing else. And they will continue to use it as a tension reliever—essentially at night before falling asleep, perhaps in daytime tension-producing situations as well. (If there is a great deal of daytime thumb sucking, it is a good idea to look into what is making the youngster bored, tired, anxious, or unhappy.)

You may find thumb sucking personally annoying and unpleasant to watch. But it *is* a normal activity, and by and large creates no problems whatever—up to a point. The sole reason for being concerned about continued thumb sucking, from a medical standpoint, is that a vigorous sucker can easily—and often does—push his upper front teeth outward. Even that is not a cause for profound concern if it's his baby teeth that are involved; if the sucking stops, they'll move back into line within a couple of months. So long as his second teeth have not yet appeared, no permanent damage will be done. But if a child is still sucking his thumb—even if it's only at night—when the permanent teeth are preparing to erupt, then the habit is quite properly a cause for parental concern. And for action. (Of course if you can get a child to stop before that stage, all the better.)

Obviously you cannot remove a thumb as you can a pacifier. And believe me, it will not help to paint the thumb with a bad-tasting substance; a dedicated thumb sucker will simply lick it off. The only method I know that will guarantee prevention is to physically restrain the child's arms so he cannot bend them; in my view, that is cruel and inhuman.

You might, of course, try *asking* the child to stop. If nature is on your side, an appeal to his vanity may be possible. Not uncommonly, a callus forms at the base of the thumb that's sucked (usually only one thumb is favored, and the other is not used); it is generally very large and very ugly. Be assured —and assure your youngster—that it will disappear very shortly after the sucking stops.

Occasionally an infection can occur at the base of the thumb, where the child's teeth have actually broken through the skin. This may make sucking so painful for the child that he will abandon the habit of his own accord.

But if discussion by you doesn't work, and there is nothing about the thumb itself to deter the child, take the problem to your dentist. Sometimes an appeal from the dentist will work when those of the parents have not. If the thumb sucker still stands firm, and there is imminent danger of disrupting the permanent teeth at this point, your dentist may feel it necessary and desirable to insert a special device in the child's mouth that will make thumb sucking downright uncomfortable.

Tics

Tics are relatively uncommon among infants and preschoolers. Sometimes (generally in older children, rather than younger ones) they're due to emotional problems. But in the age group we're talking about, they tend to take the form of eye blinking, which is often due to unsuspected vision difficulties, or to inflammation—whether allergic or infectious—of the membranes around the eye.

What you should not do is call a child's attention to the habit. What you should do is discuss it with your doctor—and, if he or she so recommends, with an ophthalmologist (eye specialist).

14

What to Do with the Time You've Saved

At the beginning of this book I made it clear that I think
your rapport with your child takes precedence over some of
the purely mechanical chores, and I urged you to bend your
efforts in that direction—to cut down on unnecessary work
so that you could devote more of your energies to your human relationship with your youngster.

I hope the prior thirteen chapters have offered practical
pointers to that end. If you do find you have conserved precious time and energy, then the effort has been successful.

The suggestions that follow reflect my own views; they
have not been discussed with any child psychologists or psychiatrists. They are based upon both what I have seen in
some successful parent-child relationships and what I felt
was missing—and would perhaps have made the difference—
in others. I ask that you consider them, and accept or reject
them as your own inclinations dictate.

• Sing to your child. Parents used to sing to their youngsters, but it is unfortunately a dying habit; if this suggestion
helps to revive it, I shall be delighted. Sing whatever you like
to sing; babies are equally accepting of opera and blues, sea

chanties and popular love songs. Your child is not a music critic and will not know whether or not your voice is off key; he will simply know that he is an audience of one and will glow with that instinctive realization.

• When your child is old enough, tell him or her stories—stories from your own childhood (and later life), as well as stories that you may read or concoct. Especially if your ethnic or national background is other than native American, you have something special and unique to offer. I think it a shame that more parents do not relate to their offspring tales of their own experiences—wherever and whenever they may have occurred, so long as they are different from those the child is likely to have. *Every* parent can read *Peter Rabbit* and *Winnie the Pooh* to a child; *your* personal experiences are unique.

• If you are bilingual, I feel strongly that your child should learn both languages; the result can only be enriching. In one family I know, one parent is of Greek descent, the other Italian. The grandparents, who visit frequently, were born in their respective countries and prefer to speak their native tongues. So the children have been taught to communicate in all three languages. This is not only gratifying to the grandparents but stimulating for the youngsters as well.

• Share your own ongoing interests, if the child is capable of grasping them (and they might be scaled down to meet his level of understanding). Whether you are involved in museum visiting, ecology, stamp collecting, art, theater—introduce your children to what turns you on. It may turn *them* on.

• *Talk* to your child—and, just as important, *listen.* This sounds a bit fatuous, but seriously, discover what your child is thinking—and sympathize with and encourage whatever interests emerge, even if they are not yours. If your main passion is house plants, and your child evidences a strong interest in spending a good deal of time at the local zoo, which bores you to tears—well, he's not old enough to go without you, is he? Besides, *you* may learn something interesting; you never know.

• Introduce your youngster to your place of work, if you work outside your home. What may seem routine to you can really excite a child—and you may get a new outlook on your work!

• Embark on adventures together. Practically every parent I have known has had a desire to see and visit community facilities and events billed as strictly for children. Wonderful—you have your ticket of admission! Groove together.

These, I hope, will be mere starting points. To me, the first five years of a child's life are a thoroughly exciting, constantly stimulating period; I wish no less for you.

Appendix A:

The 33 Most-Asked Questions:
A Check List for New Parents

First-time parents invariably have questions—frequently, questions that will seem ridiculous the second time around but can really bother the brand-new mother and father. It is my custom, when I first meet the parents of a new patient who is a first child, to sit down with them and invite them to ask whatever is on their minds. What follows—in no special order—are the questions I have heard repeatedly from new parents over the years, the dilemmas voiced as often today as they were a decade or two ago.

If you have "beginner" questions that are not answered here, you should discuss them with your own doctor.

Q. *What do I do if the baby has hiccoughs?*
A. Ignore them. Frequent hiccoughs are universal in the newborn period; many mothers, in fact, have reported feeling them even before the baby was born. There is nothing you need do about them, because hiccoughs do not upset an infant as they do older children and adults. Remember that if he *were* in distress he would cry.

Q. *When can I take the baby out?*
A. If he was born in the hospital, and you took him home, you have already taken him out. Next question. (And see Chapter 6 for further comment.)

Q. *Is air conditioning all right for the baby?*
A. Chances are, the hospital nursery in which he spent his first days was air-conditioned. His mother's room, however, may not have been so equipped, and the baby was moved back and forth without any ill effects.

Q. *Why are his hands and feet so cold?*
A. All babies' hands and feet are cold, simply because their circulation isn't yet efficient enough to keep their extremities as warm as the rest of the body. You do not need to cover them. If, in fact, you attempt to keep them as warm as the rest of his body, he is likely to develop prickly heat—even in the middle of winter.

Q. *Why is his breathing so noisy sometimes and so quiet at other times?*
A. Sometimes his nose gets stuffed, which makes for noisy breathing. So does yours. If you are awake, you will probably blow it—something that babies cannot do. If you are sleeping, your breathing will be noisy. More people snore than people think.

Q. *How many stools a day are normal for a baby?*
A. None, twelve, or some number in between, depending on the baby (see pages 41–42).

Q. *Should I give the baby water?*
A. Most babies do not like it and will refuse it except when they are very thirsty—i.e., when they are very hot. The rest of the time, the baby is hungry. Remember that he takes his nourishment in liquid form; milk or formula is about 87 percent water.

Q. *When can the baby travel by car? by plane? by bus?*
A. I think the confines of a plane or bus may be a bit difficult to manage, but a good deal depends on the length of the trip and the frequency with which the child must be fed, changed, etc. It is, in short, a practical question rather than a medical one; the travel per se, whatever the means, will not harm the child, no matter how young he is. I have had several patients who were adopted and were flown to New York from the West Coast at the age of five days.

Q. *Are babies immune to colds?*
A. If they were, we would be spending a lot of our time trying to package whatever secret ingredient rendered them so. Babies are immune—for a few months—to certain ills to which their mothers are immune; the protection finds its way into the baby's circulation during pregnancy and persists for a while. Since no adult females can claim immunity to colds, this means that babies are just as susceptible to colds as anyone else, in fact possibly *more* so.

Q. *How will I know when the baby is sick?*
A. Believe me, *you will know*. He will behave in some obviously peculiar manner. Or you will have the gut feeling that something is wrong, although you may not be able to put your finger on precisely what it is; you will probably be right, and a call to the doctor is in order.

Q. *Does the baby need a hat to go out?*
A. If it is very cold weather, cold enough for *you* to need a hat, yes. If it is very hot and sunny, and the baby has a scanty growth of fairly light hair, yes. Otherwise, no.

Q. *How much sleep does the baby need?*
A. Maybe ten hours a day, maybe twenty-three, probably some amount in between. Whatever it is, he will get it. See Chapter 4 for a full discussion.

Q. *Can I overfeed the baby?*
A. No. Every baby will stop sucking when he is full, and you won't be able to get another drop into him. If you attempt to force food into him beyond this point, he will only vomit.

Q. *Can I underfeed the baby?*
A. Yes, if you refuse him food when he is hungry; most babies make such a racket when they are hungry that it is difficult, if not impossible, to ignore.

Q. *Does it mean the baby's nervous if his jaw quivers or his hands and feet shake?*
A. No. These trembles are common during the early months. Like other parts of the baby's body, his nervous system isn't fully developed yet; various stimuli—ranging from a new and exciting event to a breath of cool air—can set off exaggerated reactions. They will lessen as the baby gets older.

Q. *How often should I burp the baby?*
A. As often as he seems to need it (see pages 17–18).

Q. *When can I start solid foods?*
A. Whenever your doctor advises (see pages 21–22 for further comment).

Q. *My newborn baby coughs and sneezes. Does he already have a cold?*
A. I certainly hope not. It's possible. But it's just as possible —and probable, since you and the hospital staff have undoubtedly been careful to guard him from contagion—that he is clearing normally accumulated mucus from his nose and throat. As I noted earlier, he cannot blow his nose. If the baby were unable to cough and sneeze, he would have no way of getting rid of excess secretions.

Q. *How close can people come to my new baby?*
A. For the first month or so, I think you are asking for trou-

ble if you allow large numbers of people to handle your new infant. I would limit the baby's contacts to those perfectly healthy people among your intimates. And, I might add, there is no reason to expose your first-born to *any child* under the age of five (obviously this protection is not possible for the second and subsequent children); I wouldn't allow a visiting child within six feet of the new baby.

Q. *What should I do with the navel when the cord comes off?*
A. Keep it clean and help it to heal (specifics, on pages 75 and 79).

Q. *Should I have my baby boy circumcised?*
A. It's entirely up to you. The only medical indication for circumcision is a condition called phimosis, which means a tightly adherent foreskin. Since the foreskins of all newborn boys are adherent, you should discuss with your doctor whether this one is likely to pose a future problem. Otherwise, I think it is a matter for the parents themselves to decide. If you have no strong feelings either way, you might wish to have him circumcised if his father is and leave him alone if his father is not, since little boys tend to identify with their fathers.

Q. *What should I do about the circumcision?*
A. Nothing in particular; it will heal by itself within a few days (and will look swollen and yellowish—which is normal, and no cause for alarm). The baby is not in any pain whatever. Usually the obstetrician or other individual who performed the circumcision will have applied a lubricated gauze dressing, and may have suggested that you continue to apply such dressings. Personally, I find that unnecessary; I generally tell parents they need not replace the initial dressing when it falls off, and I find that healing proceeds perfectly well without it.

If your son has not been circumcised, on the other hand, there *are* things you should do (see pages 79–80).

Q. *Why are the baby's breasts swollen?*
A. This sometimes happens a few days after birth; there may even be a brief release of a semi-watery, semi-milky fluid from the nipples. It's caused by a little of the mother's hormones' slipping into the baby's circulation, and it will go away and should not be worried about.

Q. *How will I know if the baby wants his pacifier or more milk?*
A. Often, you won't. Make a guess; you have a fifty-fifty chance of being right, and he will reject what you offer if it's not what he had in mind (more on this, page 19).

Q. *How often should I bathe the baby? How often should his head be washed?*
A. His head should be washed once a week. The rest of him does not need such frequent cleansing, although he might well like it (see Chapter 5 for full discussion).

Q. *Can I hurt the "soft spot"?*
A. Only if you go at it with malicious intent, using an ice pick or other sharp instrument; otherwise, it is not likely (see pages 75–76).

Q. *When is the weather too bad for the baby to go out?*
A. It is never too cold, too rainy, too snowy, too sleety, or too windy for the baby to go out, even though *you* may prefer not to go out; he will always be adequately protected from the elements. It may, however, be too hot and humid for him outdoors (for further comment, see pages 99–102).

Q. *How will I know if the baby is too lightly dressed? Or overdressed?*
A. In the first instance, if he bawls and/or turns blue. In the

second, a much more frequent occurrence, only by the results
—e.g., prickly heat or total collapse (see Chapter 6 for further
comment).

Q. *Should I swaddle the baby?*
A. Some like it; some don't. You might try, and see which
way your baby feels.

Q. *Why does he spit so much?*
A. He is probably a baby who does not burp a lot. Some babies swallow air from around the nipple only in very tiny
amounts, and it may take some time for these little bubbles
to coalesce into something large enough to bring up. At that
point, any milk sitting on top of that big bubble may come
up as well. And the baby "spits up."

Q. *Does it destroy the breast milk supply if I give occasional
bottles?*
A. No, on the contrary (notes for novices on this and other
aspects of breast feeding, pages 8–11).

Q. *Will we spoil the baby if we pick him up whenever he
cries?*
A. *Absolutely not* (see pages 104–7 for a full discussion).

Q. *Should we hire a baby nurse for the first few weeks?*
A. That's up to you. Personally, I don't think so. Many
(though by no means all) baby nurses are officious and intimidating and tend to make you feel less, rather than more,
secure in your handling of your baby. Caring for a newborn
infant is not all that difficult, anyway; just learn to nap when
the baby does. What you *can* use to advantage during these
first weeks is someone—whether friend, relative, or hired help
—to lend a hand with household chores and protect you from
being disturbed by well-meaning callers and visitors when
you are trying to rest.

Appendix B:

Other Helpful Reading

The literature is full of advice books, and if you attempt to go through even a fraction of them you will be thoroughly confused and you will have no time to do anything else. I have deliberately kept this list extremely short. The works listed cover the various aspects of what you need to know in authoritative, accurate, and readable fashion. There is no reason for parents to burden themselves with books not related to their own child—and your own physician is probably in a better position to advise you than most of the books on the market.

These are my own highly personal selections. Unless I've indicated otherwise, they are available at, or may be ordered through, bookstores.

The Mothers' Medical Encyclopedia, by Virginia E. Pomeranz, M.D., and Dodi Schultz. Signet/New American Library, 1972 (paperback). An all-inclusive cradle-through-college reference book, covering all common (and many uncommon) ills, emergency first-aid procedures, drugs and medications, definitions of medical terms, growth and development, immunizations, teething.

A Child's Mind, by Muriel Beadle. Doubleday, 1970. Subtitled "How Children Learn During the Critical Years from Birth to Age Five," this is a highly informative and very read-

The First Five Years

able review of what is known of the subject, by a thorough researcher and lucid writer. Ms. Beadle explains in fascinating detail many of the perceptual peculiarities of infants and toddlers to which I have necessarily referred only briefly.

The Wonderful Story of How You Were Born, by Sidonie Matsner Gruenberg. Doubleday, 1971 (new edition). Designed to be read by children of nine or ten, but an excellent guide for shy parents who are at a loss for words and ideas in explaining the subject to a younger child.

What Every Child Would Like His Parents to Know to Help with the Emotional Problems of His Everyday Life, by Dr. Lee Salk. McKay, 1972. A leading child psychologist deals authoritatively with dilemmas ranging from the selection of a baby-sitter and coping with grandparents to communication of the facts of death and divorce.

What to Buy in Child Restraint Systems. National Highway Traffic Safety Administration, 1971; 20¢.* A must for the parent who takes his or her child driving, this booklet clears up the widespread confusion on what types of car beds, seats, straps, etc., are safe and necessary for the infant and preschooler—and, as important, which are *unsafe.*

Fire Extinguishers. General Services Administration, 1971; 40¢.* Revealing in clear, nontechnical terms, what the government has learned in purchasing its own equipment, and spelling out how to select the correct kinds of extinguishers for your home.

If your youngster has some special medical problem that is not covered—or covered in insufficient detail—in the first book on this list, and you would like further information, there are two possible sources.

* At Government Printing Office bookstores in Atlanta; Birmingham, Ala.; Boston; Canton, Ohio; Chicago; Dallas; Denver; Detroit; Kansas City, Mo.; Los Angeles; New York City; Philadelphia; San Francisco—or by mail (check or money order must be enclosed) from the Superintendent of Documents, U.S. Government Printing Office, Washington, D.C. 20402.

One is the Government Printing Office in Washington (see the footnote on the preceding page); request the current price list of consumer publications, which may include literature on the subject.

A second may be a nonprofit organization devoted to dispensing just such information, if your child's condition is one of those for which such a group has been formed. Among such organizations are:

Allergy Foundation of America, 801 Second Avenue, New York, N.Y. 10017

National Cystic Fibrosis Research Foundation, 202 East 44th Street, New York, N.Y. 10017

National Kidney Foundation, 315 Park Avenue South, New York, N.Y. 10010

American Diabetes Association, 18 East 48th Street, New York, N.Y. 10017

National Association of Hearing and Speech Agencies, 919 18th Street, Washington, D.C. 20006

Muscular Dystrophy Association of America, 1790 Broadway, New York, N.Y. 10019

National Association for Retarded Children, 2709 Avenue E, East, Arlington, Texas 76010

National Hemophilia Foundation, 25 West 39th Street, New York, N.Y. 10018

Epilepsy Foundation of America, 1828 L Street, N.W., Washington, D.C. 20036

United Cerebral Palsy, 66 East 34th Street, New York, N.Y. 10016

Arthritis Foundation, 1212 Avenue of the Americas, New York, N.Y. 10036

Deafness Research Foundation, 366 Madison Avenue, New York, N.Y. 10017

American Foundation for the Blind, 15 West 16th Street, New York, N.Y. 10011

Index